Designing Water Disaster Management Policies

This book represents a landmark effort to probe and analyze the theory and empirics of designing water disaster management policies. It consists of seven chapters that examine, in-depth and comprehensively, issues that are central to crafting effective policies for water disaster management. The authors use historical surveys, institutional analysis, econometric investigations, empirical case studies, and conceptual-theoretical discussions to clarify and illuminate the complex policy process.

The specific topics studied in this book include a review and analysis of key policy areas and research priority areas associated with water disaster management, community participation in disaster risk reduction, the economics and politics of 'green' flood control, probabilistic flood forecasting for flood risk management, polycentric governance and flood risk management, drought management with the aid of dynamic inter-generational preferences, and how social resilience can inform SA/SIA for adaptive planning for climate change in vulnerable areas.

A unique feature of this book is its analysis of the causes and consequences of water disasters and efforts to address them successfully through policy-rich, cross-disciplinary and transnational papers. This book is designed to help enrich the sparse discourse on water disaster management policies and galvanize water professionals to craft creative solutions to tackle water disasters efficiently, equitably, and sustainably. This book should also be of consider able use to disaster management professionals, in general, and natural resource policy analysts.

This book was published as a special issue of the *Journal of Natural Resource Policy Research*.

Chennat Gopalakrishnan is Professor (Emeritus) of Natural Resource Economics at the University of Hawaii. He has published seven books and approximately 115 journal articles and technical papers on current and emerging issues in natural resource economics and policy. He is a fellow of the American Water Resources Association and International Water Resources Association and a Distinguished Scholar of the Western Agricultural Economics Association.

Designing Water Disaster Management Policies

Theory and empirics

Edited by
Chennat Gopalakrishnan

Routledge
Taylor & Francis Group

LONDON AND NEW YORK

First published 2016 by Routledge

2 Park Square, Milton Park, Abingdon, Oxon OX14 4RN
711 Third Avenue, New York, NY 10017, USA

Routledge is an imprint of the Taylor & Francis Group, an informa business

First issued in paperback 2017

British Library Cataloguing in Publication Data
A catalogue record for this book is available from the British Library

ISBN 13: 978-1-138-93079-7 (hbk)
ISBN 13: 978-1-138-08539-8 (pbk)

Typeset in Times New Roman
by RefineCatch Limited, Bungay, Suffolk

Publisher's Note
The publisher accepts responsibility for any inconsistencies that may have
arisen during the conversion of this book from journal articles to book chapters,
namely the possible inclusion of journal terminology.

Disclaimer
Every effort has been made to contact copyright holders for their permission to
reprint material in this book. The publishers would be grateful to hear from any
copyright holder who is not here acknowledged and will undertake to rectify
any errors or omissions in future editions of this book.

Contents

Citation Information

The chapters in this book were originally published in the *Journal of Natural Resources Policy Research*, volume 7, issue 1 (January 2015). When citing this material, please use the original page numbering for each article, as follows:

Chapter 1
Introduction: designing water disaster management policies: theory and empirics
Chennat Gopalakrishnan
Journal of Natural Resources Policy Research, volume 7, issue 1 (January 2015)
pp. 1–4

Chapter 2
Flood disaster management policy: an analysis of the United States Community Ratings System
Abdul-Akeem Sadiq and Douglas S. Noonan
Journal of Natural Resources Policy Research, volume 7, issue 1 (January 2015)
pp. 5–22

Chapter 3
A historical examination of the Corps of Engineers and natural valley storage protection: the economics and politics of 'green' flood control
Carolyn Kousky
Journal of Natural Resources Policy Research, volume 7, issue 1 (January 2015)
pp. 23–40

Chapter 4
Probabilistic forecasting and the reshaping of flood risk management
Sarah Michaels
Journal of Natural Resources Policy Research, volume 7, issue 1 (January 2015)
pp. 41–52

Chapter 5
Examining the benefits of collaboration: the Provider-User Matrix for collaborative flood risk management illustrated by the case of the Ljusnan River, Sweden
Beatrice Hedelin and Mattias Hjerpe
Journal of Natural Resources Policy Research, volume 7, issue 1 (January 2015)
pp. 53–70

Chapter 6

Adapting to catastrophic water scarcity in agriculture through social networking and inter-generational occupational transitioning
Ram Ranjan
Journal of Natural Resources Policy Research, volume 7, issue 1 (January 2015) pp. 71–92

Chapter 7

Can social resilience inform SA/SIA for adaptive planning for climate change in vulnerable regions?
Allan Dale, Karen J. Vella, and Alison Cottrell
Journal of Natural Resources Policy Research, volume 7, issue 1 (January 2015) pp. 93–104

For any permission-related enquiries please visit: http://www.tandfonline.com/page/help/permissions

Contributors

Alison Cottrell, James Cook University, Australia

Allan Dale, James Cook University, Australia

Chennat Gopalakrishnan, University of Hawaii, USA

Beatrice Hedelin, Karlstad University, Sweden

Mattias Hjerpe, Linkoping University, Sweden

Carolyn Kousky, Resources for the Future, USA

Sarah Michaels, University of Nebraska, USA

Douglas S. Noonan, Indiana University-Purdue University Indianapolis, USA

Ram Ranjan, Macquarie University, Australia

Abdul-Akeem Sadiq, Indiana University-Purdue University Indianapolis, USA

Karen J. Vella, Griffith University, Australia

Introduction: designing water disaster management policies: theory and empirics

Chennat Gopalakrishnan

Department of Natural Resources and Environmental Management, University of Hawaii, Honolulu, HI, USA

The human and economic impacts of water disasters have increased dramatically in recent years. This is evidenced by the fact that they contributed to nearly 90% of all natural disasters, 96% of the people affected (2.4 billion) and 76% of the economic damages (approximately USD 1 trillion) caused by natural disasters globally. Despite the conspicuous presence of water disasters, discourse on their policy aspects continues to remain a neglected area (for a detailed analysis, see Gopalakrishnan, 2013).

Ossified governance structures, polycentric decision-making entities, entropy-ridden institutions, cascading conflict scenarios, deep-seated and wide-ranging internal feuds and precariously perched, top-heavy decision agencies significantly add to the complexity of policy domains in the water disasterscape. Such an intractable combination of essentially incompatible forces and features renders the design and implementation of effective and efficient disaster risk management policies an extraordinarily challenging proposition. Against this bleak backdrop, well-intentioned policies stumble into a collision course, making the emergence of workable policies exceedingly difficult. The purpose of this special issue is to help identify, examine, analyze and assess the complex world of disaster management, and design robust, effective, implementation-friendly, widely-accessible and affordable policies.

Based on a historical survey of natural disasters in general, and water disasters in particular, I have identified five broad categories of water policies for an in-depth study: risk management; vulnerability assessment; capacity building and resilience; disaster risk reduction-development linkage; and institutional design (see Table 1) (Gopalakrishnan, 2013).

Table 1. Policy Areas (PA) and Research Priority Areas (RPA) identified in Gopalakrishnan's paper*.

Policy Areas (PA)	Research Priority Areas (RPA)
Risk management	Reliable database
Vulnerability assessment	Climate-induced vulnerability
Capacity building and resilience	Capacity building and resilience
Disaster risk reduction-development linkage	Mainstreaming disaster risk reduction policies
Institutional design	Effective implementation policies grounded in new institutions

*Chennat Gopalakrishnan (2013).
Table developed by the author based on information presented in this paper.

1

A review of the literature pertaining to these policy areas shows only a modest record of success in terms of actual performance. And my analysis shows considerable scope for further improvement in each of these areas. What follows is a brief discussion of the performance of each policy area over an extended period in the past. A review of risk management shows instance after instance of failure in the implementation of disaster management projects, resulting in widespread destruction. Floods, droughts, and wind-storms (88.5% of the 1000 most disastrous events) continue to cause major destruction and human casualties in many parts of the world, most notably, Asia (Adikari & Yoshianti, 2009). The Intergovernmental Panel on Climate Change (IPCC) projects that global climate change will significantly add to water-related risks in the years to come (Bates, Kundzewiez, & Palutikof, 2008). This calls for a far more effective implementation of risk management policies. In the case of vulnerability assessment, only limited attention has been paid to the potential for exacerbation of climate-driven disaster impacts (human casualties, economic losses, and environmental disruptions) in urban and rural areas, especially in developing countries.

My review suggests that there is limited understanding of the concept of disaster resilience among disaster policy makers, the main reason for the shortage of concrete examples of the adoption of resilience-enhancing measures by many countries and regions affected by water disasters. Another critical policy area is closely allied to the linkage between disaster risk reduction and development. However, the link between the two has not been recognized in most of the current plans, for example, the Millennium Development Plan and the Hyogo Framework. To reduce the impact of water disasters on sustainable development, it is critical to craft new policies clearly acknowledging the link between disaster risk reduction and development (Askew, 1997). The final area of concern in water disaster policy relates to the role of water institutions. Historical data and empirical evidence gleaned from national and international sources point to several instances of dysfunctional institutions engaged in water disaster management at the global, regional, national, state and local levels (Gopalakrishnan & Okada, 2007, 2012; Kreimer, 2002; Mileti, 1999; Zimmerman & Cusker, 2001).

Against this backdrop, I have examined each of the above policy areas with a view to thoroughly revamp them, in order to enable them to efficiently and effectively incorporate the continuing advances in the disaster management field. Furthermore, based on this review, a number of specific recommendations were made for timely incorporation in the policies as they were being crafted. The key suggested changes include 'a comprehensive disaster risk assessment policy, an effective early-warning system, a carefully-crafted vulnerability assessment and reduction system, capacity building and resilience enhance-ment measures, integration of water disaster risk reduction policies into development plans at all levels, and revamping of water institutions through "institutional entropy" reduction measures' (Gopalakrishnan, 2013, p. 268).

Based on the information and insights gained from the examination of the policy areas discussed above, it became clear that there were egregious gaps that needed to be filled in order to develop research-grounded policies. Noted below are the five priority areas for research that I have identified in order to accomplish this task: (1) a reliable database; (2) climate-induced vulnerability; (3) capacity building and resilience; (4) mainstreaming disaster risk reduction; and (5) effective implementation policies grounded in new institu-tions (Gopalakrishnan, 2013) (see Table 1).

This special issue, so far as we know, is a first attempt to bring together a collection (six in all) of original papers which examine in-depth and comprehensively the theoretical and

Table 2. Policy Areas (PA) and Research Priority Areas (RPA) addressed in special issue papers.

Author(s)	Policy Areas (PA)	Research Priority Areas (RPA)
Sadiq and Noonan	(Flood) Risk management, resilience, disaster risk reduction-development linkage	Reliable database, mainstreaming disaster risk reduction policies, resilience
Kousky	(Flood) Risk management, institutional design	Reliable database, policies grounded in new institutions
Michaels	(Flood) Risk management	Reliable database
Hedelin and Hjerpe	(Flood) Risk management	Reliable database, policies grounded in new institutions
Ranjan	(Drought) Vulnerability, Resilience	Reliable database, resilience, climate-induced vulnerability
Dale, Vella and Cottrell	Vulnerability, resilience	Reliable database, climate-induced vulnerability, resilience

empirical dimensions of water disaster management policies. The first four papers – Sadiq and Noonan; Kousky; Michaels; and Hedelin and Hjerpe (Table 2) – focus on the policy areas (PA) of (flood) risk management, resilience, and disaster risk reduction-development linkage, while the fifth paper by Ranjan addresses drought-induced vulnerability and resilience, with the sixth and final paper by Dale, Vella, and Cottrell devoted to a review and analysis of resilience, in the context of climate-triggered vulnerability. All six papers also contribute to several Research Priority Areas (RPAs) in some measure (see Table 2).

A brief discussion of each of the papers included in this special issue follows. In the opening paper, Sadiq and Noonan discuss and evaluate the efficiency of the United States Community Ratings System (CRS) in encouraging community participation in disaster risk reduction activities. Through a national level analysis, the authors identify the motivating factors behind the community's voluntary participation and intensity of participation in the CRS. The study results provide insights into the factors that are important predictors of community participation in a voluntary national program designed to minimize community flood losses and to make communities more resilient to flood disasters. In the next paper, Kousky discusses the economics and politics of 'green' flood control through a detailed examination of the issues connected with the purchase of 8500 acres of wetlands in New England by the US Army Corps of Engineers for flood protection in the 1970s. The studies by the Corps of Engineers, carried out between 1970 and 1992, raised serious questions (except in one case) about the desirability and feasibility of acquiring large tracts of land by a federal agency for the protection of natural valley storage (NVS) areas.

Michaels, in the third paper, examines from a practitioner perspective some crucial issues associated with the current state of incorporating probabilistic flood forecasting in flood-risk management. The author points out how uncertainty articulated in forecasts can be made useful to practitioners through interpretation and constructive use, identifies four emerging trends to watch, and discusses the technical challenges involved in using 'ensemble prediction systems' for flood forecasts. In the next paper, Hedelin and Hjerpe probe and analyze the benefits of collaboration in flood-risk management through a study of a Provider-User Matrix, illustrated by the case of the Ljusnan River (LRJ) in Sweden. The authors, in this case study of the benefits of polycentric governance, make a strong case for the application of comprehensive and context-based approaches toward collaboration.

The focus now shifts from flood-risk management to drought management, especially of the climate-induced variety, which takes on urgency in view of the potential of droughts for colossal impacts on the rural communities. Ranjan, in his paper, addresses in detail the issue of adapting to catastrophic water scarcity in agriculture with the aid of a model of dynamic inter-generational preferences and occupational choices that explores possible transition paths out of agriculture.

In the final article, Dale, Vella and Cottrell examine to what extent social resilience can inform SA (social assessment)/SIA (social impact assessment) for adaptive planning for climate change in vulnerable regions. The authors note the growing importance of social resilience concepts in environmental planning, discuss the disconnect between the ecological and social science perspectives of resilience, based on an extensive literature review, and recommend cross-disciplinary interaction to enhance their effectiveness in dealing with climate change adaptation.

We hope that this special issue will receive the attention of all those who are responsible for conceiving, developing and implementing water disaster management policies at the local, national, regional and global levels. The conceptual-theoretical analyses, the empirical studies and the case histories included in it should help enrich the discourse on water disaster management policies, and hopefully, inspire all concerned parties to craft creative solutions to tackling water disasters effectively, efficiently, and equitably.

References

Adikari, Y., & Yoshianti, J. (2009). *Global trends in water-related disasters: An insight for policy-makers*. Paris, France: UN World Water Assessment Programme.

Askew, A. J. 1997. Water in the international decade for natural disaster reduction. In G. H. Leavesley, H. F. Lins, F. Nobilis, R. S. Parker, V. R. Schneider & F. H. M. Van de Ven (Eds.), *Destructive water: Water-caused natural disaster, their abatement and control* (pp. 3–11). Wallingford, UK: IAHS Press.

Bates, B. C., Kundzewiez, Z. W. & Palutikof, J. P. (Eds.). (2008). *Climate change and water*. Technical paper of IPCC. Geneva: IPCC Secretariat.

Gopalakrishnan, C., & Okada, N. (2007). Designing new institutions for implementing integrated disaster risk management: Key elements and future directions. *Disasters, 31*(4), 353–372. doi:10.1111/j.1467-7717.2007.01013.x

Gopalakrishnan, C., & Okada, N. (2012). Reflections on implementation science. *Journal of Natural Resources Policy Research, 4*(1), 79–88. doi:10.1080/19390459.2012.652822

Gopalakrishnan, C. (2013). Water and disasters: A review and analysis of policy aspects. *International Journal of Water Resources Development, 29*, 2, 250–271. doi:10.1080/07900627.2012.756133

Kreimer, A. (2002, April 25). 'Disaster management in metropolitan areas'. World Bank Metropolitan Governance Series. Retrived from http://www.Worldbank.org.WBI/B-SPAN/docs/metrogovernanceI.pdf

Mileti, D. (1999). *Disasters by design: A reassessment of natural hazards in the united states*. Washington, DC: Joseph Henry Press.

Zimmerman, R., & Cusker, M. (2001, July). "Institutional decision-making," Chapter 9 & Appendix 10. In C. Rosenzweig & W. D. Solecki (Eds.), *Climate change and a global city: The potential consequences of climate variability and change* (pp. 9-1 to 9-25 and A11-A17). Metro east coast. New York, NY: Columbia Earth Institute & Goddard Institute of Space Studies.

Flood disaster management policy: an analysis of the United States Community Ratings System

Abdul-Akeem Sadiq and Douglas S. Noonan

School of Public and Environmental Affairs, Indiana University-Purdue University Indianapolis, Indianapolis, IN, USA

In 1990 the US Federal Emergency Management Agency created the Community Ratings System (CRS) to engage local governments to enhance community flood resilience. The CRS encourages community flood risk management activities by discounting flood insurance premiums commensurate with the level of flood management measures implemented. Using a national sample of communities, this study empirically identifies factors motivating both communities' decision to participate and intensity of participation in the CRS. The results indicate that local capacity, flood risk factors, socio-economic characteristics, and political economy factors are significant predictors of CRS participation. Further, factors predicting participation in the CRS differ from factors predicting CRS scores.

1. Introduction

Water disaster management in the United States (US), and flood disaster management in particular, generally involves both local and national-level policies and institutions. Much can be learned from analyzing the US experience with improving its flood disaster management. Historically, the US has suffered considerable losses, both in terms of lives lost and property damage, to flooding events. For example, the 30-year average for flood-related deaths and flood damage from 1982 to 2011 are 95 fatalities and $8.20 billion, respectively (National Weather Services [NWS], 2013). The devastation caused by flooding is also reflected in Presidential Disaster Declarations, where over 80% of presidentially declared disaster losses are engendered by flooding (Landry & Li, 2012). As a result of persistent increases in flood losses and the unavailability of private flood insurance (Federal Emergency Management Agency [FEMA], 2011), the federal government passed the National Flood Insurance Act (NFIA) in 1968, which established the National Flood Insurance Program (NFIP). One of the goals of the NFIP is to reduce future flood losses by encouraging communities to adopt and enforce floodplain management ordinances in exchange for federally backed flood insurance (FEMA, 2011). As of December 2011, approximately 5.6 million residential and commercial insurance policies were in force, totaling $1.26 trillion in coverage (FEMA, 2013). Although the NFIP has been successful in providing support to flood victims, some argue that the NFIP subsidized insurance premiums may be encouraging more losses or development in high-risk areas (e.g., Goodwin, 2013; Kousky & Kunreuther, 2013; Thomas & Leichenko, 2011). In order to reduce flood losses, which are still substantial (FEMA, 2013), in 1990, the FEMA created the Community Ratings System (CRS) through the NFIP. CRS is a voluntary program that encourages communities to engage in additional flood risk management activities by offering communities discounted flood insurance premiums commensurate with the level of flood management measures implemented.

The relatively new CRS marked a departure in using a federal program (NFIP) to directly engage local governments in integrating flood risk reduction into their plans and to enhance community flood resilience. Better understanding CRS performance promises to respond, in part, to two of the five research priority areas identified in Gopalakrishnan (2013): mainstreaming risk reduction policies and capacity building and resilience. Although researchers have studied the factors that motivate communities to participate in the CRS within single states (Brody, Zahran, Highfield, Bernhardt, & Vedlitz, 2009; Landry & Li, 2012), there is only one study to our knowledge on the factors that motivate communities to participate in the CRS for a national sample. Previous research into the factors motivating participation in the CRS typically looked only at single state case studies and did not assess the 'intensity' of participation as measured by the CRS scores. Results for particular state case studies may not generalize well to the nation as a whole. We examine participation of cities, towns, villages, and townships across the nation. Further, participation and the intensity of participation are closely linked community decisions yet have different determinants. As a result, this study attempts to empirically answer two questions: (1) what factors motivate communities to participate in the CRS? (2) What factors predict CRS scores conditional on CRS participation? A good under-standing of what factors motivate communities to not only participate in the CRS, but also attain high CRS scores can help policy makers to develop targeted policies to address flood risks and subsequently reduce flood losses. Using national data on historical CRS participation, the 1990 Census, financial data from the 1992 Census of Governments, climate and topographical information from the United States Department of Agriculture (USDA), and other data sources, we analyze the determinants of CRS participation and CRS scores. We estimate two basic empirical models: (1) a logit model to explain why some communities opt to participate and others do not; (2) a tobit model and a Cragg (double-hurdle) model to explain the CRS score achieved, given that the community participated. We use these models to test several competing hypotheses – local govern-ment capacity, flood risk factors, socio-demographic factors, and political economy factors – that explain why communities participate as they do. The results indicate that local capacity, flood risk factors, socio-demographic characteristics, and political economy factors are significant predictors of CRS participation. In addition, the results indicate that the factors that motivate communities to participate in the CRS are not the same factors that predict CRS scores.

After a brief background description of the NFIP and CRS, we present a review of relevant literature followed by a discussion of the methodological approach, including the dataset used to answer the research questions. Next, we present our findings and discuss the results. Finally, we conclude with policy implications of our results and outline an agenda for future research on community flood risk mitigation.

1.1 The national flood insurance program

The recognition of the potential consequences of flooding prompted the US federal government to initially engage in structural mitigation measures – levees, seawalls, dams, among others – to control flooding and provide relief assistance to disaster victims

(FEMA, 2011). However, this strategy was neither successful in reducing flood losses nor discouraging communities from building in flood-prone areas (Brody, Kang, & Bernhardt, 2010; FEMA, 2011). To make matters worse, the private market was not providing affordable flood insurance for water damage from flooding and other storms because of the seasonality of floods, uncertainty of flood risk, and high flood risk (FEMA, 2011; Kousky, Olmstead, Walls, Stern, & Macauley, 2011; Kunreuther, 1996). Due to the increasing disaster losses and unavailability of insurance coverage from the private sector, on 1 August 1968, the US Congress established the NFIP through the passage of the NFIA, to provide flood insurance to communities. Communities can participate in the NFIP by adopting and enforcing floodplain management ordinances in exchange for federally backed flood insurance (FEMA, 2011).

In addition to providing flood insurance to communities, the NFIP also develops Flood Insurance Rate Maps (FIRM), which depict the base flood elevations, flood zones, and floodplain boundaries of the nation's communities. FIRMs help homeowners/renters and insurance companies identify flood risks (FEMA, 2002). Recognizing that buildings constructed prior to the adoption of FIRM were not likely to have known about flood risks, pre-FIRM buildings receive subsidized insurance rates. In exchange for subsidized insurance rates for pre-FIRM buildings, communities are expected to protect new construction from floods by implementing floodplain management ordinances (FEMA, 2002).

There have been several amendments to the NFIP since its creation in 1968. Realizing that communities were not participating in the NFIP at high rates voluntarily, Congress added the Mandatory Flood Insurance Purchase Requirement in 1973. This amendment mandates ' … federally insured or regulated lenders … to require flood insurance on all grants and loans for acquisition or construction of buildings in designated Special Flood Hazard Areas (SFHAs) in communities that participate in the NFIP' (FEMA, 2002, p. 3). An SFHA is a piece of land in a floodplain that has a 1% or greater chance of flooding in any given year (also known as the 100-year flood occurrence) (FEMA, 2002). This 1973 requirement engendered an increase in the number of communities participating in the NFIP from 2200 in 1973 to 15,000 in 1977 (FEMA, 2002). In 1994, the National Flood Insurance Reform Act (NFIRA) added additional measures to increase compliance of the mandatory purchase requirement, to codify the CRS, and to require the FEMA to reassess the FIRMs every five years, among other measures (FEMA, 2002). More recently, the US Congress enacted the Biggert-Waters Flood Insurance Reform and Modernization Act of 2012. Changes made by this act include premium rate structure reforms, a requirement for the FEMA to develop a reserve fund, and the development of an ongoing mapping program that will continuously update floodplain maps (National Association of Insurance Commissioners, 2012). This 2012 act was in response to recent flood disasters in the US, like Hurricane Katrina and Super storm Sandy that resulted in billions of dollars in flood damage. In the aftermath of these disasters, it was clear that many individuals had not purchased flood insurance (King, 2013). As a matter of fact, only 18% of all Americans have flood insurance (Stellin, 2012). In addition, it seems that many people misunderstand their flood risk and often underestimate the probability that a flood could occur, thereby decreasing the likelihood that they will obtain the mandatory insurance coverage (King, 2013).

1.2 The community rating system

The CRS program, which was implemented in 1990, is supposed to give additional incentives to communities to go beyond the NFIP requirements to address flood risks.

Table 1. CRS classes, credit points, and premium discounts based on location in or outside Special Flood Hazard Areas (SFHA).

		Premium Reduction	
CRS Class	Credit Points	In SFHA (%)	Outside SFHA (%)
1	4500+	45	10
2	4000–4999	40	10
3	3500–3999	35	10
4	3000–3499	30	10
5	2500–2999	25	10
6	2000–2499	20	10
7	1500–1999	15	5
8	1000–1499	10	5
9	500–999	5	5
10	0–499	0	0

Note: Extracted from FEMA (2013). National Flood Insurance Program Community Rating System Coordinator's Manual. http://www.fema.gov/media-library-data/20130726-1557-20490-9922/crs_manual_508_ok_5_10_13_book-marked.pdf

The program has three main objectives: reduce flood losses, strengthen accurate insurance ratings, and foster awareness of flood insurance (King, 2013). When communities participate in the CRS, they not only reduce their flood risks they also enjoy discounted premiums (up to 45%) on federally required flood insurance based on their community's CRS score (see Table 1). To date, over 1200 communities from all 50 states are participating voluntarily in the CRS program, achieving a wide range of ratings (FEMA, 2013). The 19 credited activities to be completed by communities fall into four major categories; public information activities, mapping and regulations, flood damage reduction activities, and warning and response (see Table 2). Public information activities promote the purchase of insurance, advise people about their flood hazards, and provide information on how to reduce risks. Mapping and regulation activities increase the protection to new development, while flood damage reduction activities address the risks present in current structures. Lastly, the warning and response activities are those that prepare communities to respond during flood events (FEMA, 2013).

2. Literature review

Improving flood disaster management policies involves better understanding current policy frameworks. Since the creation of the NFIP, researchers have studied various aspects of this program. For example, researchers have examined the problems and the potential of the NFIP (Anderson, 1974), the proposed changes for the NFIP (United States General Accounting Office (GAO), 1983), and the demand for flood insurance (Browne & Hoyt, 2000). Others have looked at the participation in the NFIP by coastal communities (Landry & Jahan-Parvar, 2011; Petrolia, Landry, & Coble, 2013) and flood risk perception in lands protected by 100-year levees (Ludy & Kondolf, 2012). Similarly, researchers have studied different aspects of the CRS. For instance, Brody et al. (2009) used the CRS as a case study to understand policy learning for flood mitigation. These researchers found that local jurisdictions do learn from histories of flood risks (Brody et al., 2009). In addition, Posey (2009) used the CRS as a proxy for adaptive capacity and examined

Table 2.   Credit points awarded for CRS activities.

Activity	Maximum Possible Points	Percent of Communities Credited[a]
300 Public Information Activities		
310 Elevation Certificates	116	100%
320 Map Information Service	90	93
330 Outreach Projects	360	90
340 Hazard Disclosure	80	68
350 Flood Protection Information	125	92
360 Flood Protection Assistance	110	41
370 Flood Insurance Promotion	110	0
400 Mapping and Regulations		
410 Floodplain Mapping	802	50%
420 Open Space Preservation	2020	68
430 Higher Regulatory Standards	2042	98
440 Flood Data Maintenance	222	87
450 Stormwater Management	755	83
500 Flood Damage Reduction Activities		
510 Floodplain Mgmt. Planning	622	43%
520 Acquisition and Relocation	1900	23
530 Flood Protection	1600	11
540 Drainage System Maintenance	570	78
600 Warning and Response		
610 Flood Warning and Response	395	37%
620 Levees	235	0
630 Dams	160	0

Note: [a]Includes communities credited partially.
Extracted from FEMA (2013). National Flood Insurance Program Community Rating System Coordinator's Manual. http://www.fema.gov/media-library-data/20130726-1557-20490-9922/crs_manual_508_ok_5_10_13_bookmarked.pdf.

whether the socio-economic status (SES) of individuals in a community is a determinant of adaptive capacity at the municipal level. Posey's results suggest an association between average individual SES and adaptive capacity of the collective (i.e., participation in the CRS) (Posey, 2009). In addition, Zahran, Weiler, Brody, and Lindell (2009) examined the correlation between flood insurance purchases by households and the flood mitigation measures implemented by local governments participating in the CRS in Florida. Their results indicate a strong correlation between household flood insurance purchase and local government mitigation activities. Furthermore, Zahran, Brody, Highfield, and Vedlitz (2010) studied the relationship between the non-linear nature of the incentive inherent in the CRS and observed changes in CRS scores. Their results indicate that adoption of mitigation measures by Florida communities are driven by the non-linear incentive nature of the CRS. Finally, Landry and Li (2012) studied the influence of local capacity, hydrological risk factors, and flood experience on community hazard mitigation decisions in North Carolina counties (participation in the CRS was used as a measure of community hazard mitigation decisions). Landry and Li's (2012) results suggest positive relationships between flood history and CRS participation, as well as between physical risk factors and CRS participation, among other findings.

Researchers have measured local capacity in terms of resource availability, such as the number of trained staff in a community (Kunreuther & Roth, 1998). Previous studies on risk reduction have established a positive relationship between resources (time, money, man-power, etc.) and adoption of risk-reducing measures at the household (Mileti, 1999), community (Brody et al., 2010; May & Birkland, 1994), and organizational levels (Dahlhamer & D'Souza, 1997; Meyer-Emerick & Momen, 2003; Mileti, Darlington, Fitzpatrick, & O'Brien, 1993; Sadiq, 2010). In the light of these findings, we expect a positive relationship between local capacity (e.g., payroll, property tax revenue, and capital outlay) and participation in the CRS.

Prior studies have measured community flood risk in several different ways depending on data availability. For example, Posey (2009) measured flood risk by the number of flood insurance policies, the amount of payments made to satisfy flood claims, and flood insurance claims filed; while Zahran et al. (2010) measure flood risk by flood frequency and flood property damage. According to the findings of these studies and others, communities that faced higher flood risks are more likely to undertake flood mitigation measures (Landry & Li, 2012; Posey, 2009; Zahran et al., 2010). As a result, we expect a positive relationship between flood risk factors (e.g., percent of community area covered by water, topography, and humidity) and participation in the CRS.

In addition, researchers have found significant relationships between socio-demographic factors – educational level, percentage of senior citizens in a community, population density – and local flood risk mitigation (Landry & Li, 2012; Zahran et al., 2010). Based on these studies, we expect a significant relationship between socio-demographic factors (e.g., educational attainment, racial composition, share of residents who are children) and CRS participation.

Landry and Li (2012) argue that wealthier communities (measured as median household income or housing values) may put less pressure on local government to adopt flood mitigation measures because they themselves undertake personal protective measures against flood. Rentership rates and the share of new residents (who likely have new mortgages governed by NFIP mandates) are also linked to local collective action. We expect a significant relationship between political economy factors (e.g., housing values, share of housing units that are rentals, household income, and turnover rates) and CRS participation.

Only one of these prior NFIP and CRS studies looks at the predictors of CRS participation using national scale data. By examining the factors that motivate communities to participate voluntarily in the CRS using national data, we hope to produce generalizable results. In addition, none of the aforementioned studies has examined whether or not the determinants of CRS participation are the same as the determinants of CRS scores. Based on our literature review and the need to contribute to this important, but scanty literature on CRS participation specifically and the study of risks in general, we posit the following hypotheses:

2.1 Hypotheses

- H1: Local capacity: communities with more financial resources (e.g., payroll, property tax revenue, and capital outlay) are more likely than communities with less financial resources to participate in the CRS and score higher CRS scores *ceteris paribus*.
- H2: Flood risk factors: communities with higher flood risks (e.g., percent of community area covered by water, topography, and humidity) are more likely than communities with lower flood risks to participate in the CRS and score higher CRS scores *ceteris paribus*.

- H3: Socio-demographic factors: the likelihood and intensity of a community's participation in the CRS is influenced by socio-demographic characteristics (e.g., educational level, racial composition, and share of residents who are children).
- H4: Political-economy factors: the likelihood and intensity of a community's participation in the CRS depends on expected capitalization gains (e.g., housing values and share of housing units that are rentals) and residents' ability to influence local policies (e.g., household income and turnover rates).

3. Methodology

3.1 Data

We combined five data sources to inform the analysis. Data on CRS participation is obtained from the 2013 *CRS Coordinator's Manual* (FEMA, 2013) and the FEMA. Underlying flood risk data from the US Department of Transportation (US DOT) (1996) offers very high resolution (1 km grid cell) rankings of flood risk (on a 0–100 scale) that use underlying topography and hydrography of the area. This flood hazard rank variable derives from a formula that equally weights annual flooding frequency ranked from 0–100 (which itself is an area-weighted average of flooding by soil map units within the 1km grid cell) and their potential scour depth ranked from 0–100. Scour depth reflects erosion hazard based on 100-year flood flow, sediment size, and stream shape character-istics (Williams, Carreon, & Bradley, 1992). Thus this flood hazard risk variable captures both the frequency and the intensity of flooding. This flood risk measure has three advantages: (1) it derives from data and computations that largely predate the start of the CRS program, (2) it offers a rich quantitative scale for flood risk, and (3) it provides spatial resolution much smaller than cities or counties, which allows better distributional characterization of flood risk[1]. The Natural Amenities Index, which contains data on the physical characteristics of counties like topography, climate, and water coverage, are taken from the USDA's Economic Research Service. Information about the population and housing stock of communities is obtained from 1990 block-group level Census data from the United States Census Bureau. Finally, information about government expendi-tures and revenues is taken from the 1992 Census of Governments, the earliest available Census data on local governments' finances.

The unit of analysis for this study is a Census place, which includes cities, towns, townships or other Census-designated places (henceforth referred to as 'places'), which captures roughly half of the CRS-participating communities. While the CRS invites participation from 'communities' – which includes both counties and incorporated cities and towns – the analysis here is restricted to places. About 4% of the 28,000-plus places in the US participate in the CRS. For some data available at the county level, each place can be associated with a host county by the United States Census Bureau (1990). This, coupled with the use of more spatially refined Census data from 1990 (i.e., block groups), enables the exploration of the broader distribution of socio-economic variables within a community (rather than relying on simple means or medians at the larger place-level). It is both possible and likely that place-average values of predictors like property values or flood risk will perform less well than peak values within the place.

All variables are taken from 1990, or as close to that year as possible, in order to better match the variables to the conditions existing before the start of the CRS program with those after, thereby enabling a causal interpretation to the findings. There is a serious concern that, for a CRS program that began in 1990, the program's operation has indeed had an impact on a host of participating places' characteristics. An effective CRS would affect flood insurance policies, claims and flood damages, and even migration and development patterns. Accordingly, relatively permanent or preexisting measures of local capacity, flood risks, socio-economic and political factors are employed in order to minimize their endogeneity in models predicting current CRS participation. A consequence of this cautious approach that predicts current participation with 'deep lags' of explanatory variables is reduced explanatory power. Significant effects in this model should be interpreted as less proximate causes of CRS participation, but rather as more indirect forces that affect participation perhaps through intermediate mechanisms (e.g., wealthier communities can better afford to start and sustain engaging a federal program). Of course, recent shocks like floods likely drive reactionary participation (Zahran et al., 2010). The influence of more permanent flood risks are captured here without including endogenous post-1990 measures like experienced flood damages or those related to flood insurance maps, policies, or claims – all of which partly result from a community's flood mitigation activities (such as CRS participation).

3.2 Variables

Table 3 shows the dependent and independent variables and their descriptions. The dependent variable for the logit model is CRS participation and the dependent variable for the tobit model and the Cragg – double hurdle model ('craggit') (Cragg, 1971) is the total CRS scores for the communities that were participating in CRS at of 2012.

3.3 Data analysis

We employ a two-stage nested model. For the participation model, we use a logit model to explain why some communities participate and others do not. Logit is an appropriate model because of the binary nature of the dependent variable. Linear probability models would yield heteroskedastic error term (Wooldridge, 2002).

To understand the predictors of CRS score conditional on participation, we use both a tobit model and a craggit model. The two-stage Cragg model offers a compelling alternative to a tobit model in this context because the tobit restricts the underlying process or parameters to be the same in determining both participation (in the first stage) and actual score (in the second stage). The craggit, which is a more flexible model than Tobit, allows for distinct processes to determine the participation and the score separately. Cragg's alternative uses a probit for the first stage and a truncated normal for the second. As the tobit model is nested in the craggit model, the Cragg approach is preferred and offers both interesting comparisons with the tobit and a useful demonstration of the value in relaxing some tobit's assumptions. The descriptive statistics for the independent and dependent variables are presented in Table 4.

4. Results

Table 4 shows that 4.2% of all communities are participating in the CRS as of 2012. This means that out of a total of 28,147 communities, 1,182 communities were participating in the CRS as at 2012. For this group of participants, the minimum CRS score obtained is 505 (CRS class 9) and the maximum CRS score obtained is 5,315 (CRS class 1). In other to determine whether there are significant differences between the means of all

Table 3.   Variable and their descriptions.

Variable	Description
Dependent variables 1. Participation in the CRS 2. Total CRS score	Communities that were participating in the CRS as of 2012 (Dichotomous: 1 for communities currently participating in the CRS and 0 for communities not currently participating in the CRS.) Total CRS score obtained by each participating community (i.e., the sum of points obtained from the 19 credited activities in Series 300, 400, 500, and 600 sections of the CRS scoring formula.)
Independent Variables	
ln(payroll)	Log of total payroll ($) for each community, 1992
PropTax	Total property tax revenue for each community, 1992
FlowCapital	Sum of annual capital outlay ($) on sewerage, solid waste management, and water transport and terminals, 1992
HousingValue	ln (county's median block-group median housing value, 1990)
HHincome	ln (county's median block-group median income, 1990)
YearBuilt	Mean of county's block group's median year housing built, 1990
RentShare	Mean of county's block group's share of housing units as rentals, 1990
StayShare	Mean of county's block group's share of households living in same home five years earlier, 1990
CollegeShare	Mean of county's block group's share with college degrees, 1990
noHSshare	Mean of county's block group's share not finishing high school, 1990
WhiteShare	Mean of county's block group's share that is white, 1990
ChildShare	Mean of county's block group's population share under age 18, 1990
Ruralness	Rural-urban continuum code from ERS (scales from 1–9, with 1 indicating counties in metro areas over 1 million population and 9 indicating completely rural counties with less than 2,500 population and no adjacent metro area)
Humidity	Average relative humidity in July
Topography	Topography code from ERS (scales from 1 for flat plains to 21 for high mountains).
Plains	Dummy variable (from *Topography*) indicating flat, smooth or irregular plains
WaterShare	Percent of county area covered by water
WaterTopo	*Water Share × Topography*
WetPlains	*Humidity × Plains*
WetTopo	*Humidity × Topography*
Floodrisk	Mean flood risk of block group with highest mean risk in county

independent variables for participant and non-participant communities, we run a t-test. The t-test results indicate that there are statistically significant differences ($p < 0.01$) between the two groups on all but three independent variables – humidity, plains, and the interaction between humidity and topography.

The logistic model is estimated using STATA statistical analysis software. Table 5 shows the results of the logistic regression. The pseudo R-square of 41.07% indicates a good fit of the logistic regression.

The result from the logistic regression indicates that local capacity factors are significant predictors of CRS participation. Specifically, the result indicates a positive

Table 4.   Descriptive statistics.

Variable	Obs.	Mean	Std. Dev.	Min	Max	Mean (CRS)[a]
Participation in CRS	28147	0.042	0.200	0	1	
Total CRS score	1174	1607.6	645.7	505	5315	
ln(payroll)	28147	8.564	2.918	0.693	20.992	12.91***
PropTax	28147	2705.011	95276.27	0	7898700	13000.42***
FlowCapital	28147	718.134	9808.715	0	729485	5554.70***
HousingValue	28147	10.879	0.441	9.461	13.122	11.19***
HHincome	28147	10.168	0.248	8.995	11.035	10.28***
YearBuilt	28147	1961.437	12.128	1714.127	1982.388	1961.30***
RentShare	28147	0.275	0.0728	0.117	0.839	0.32***
StayShare	28147	0.535	0.0773	0.217	0.783	0.46***
CollegeShare	28147	0.142	0.0627	0.034	0.505	0.18***
noHSshare	28147	0.261	0.082	0.053	0.665	0.23***
WhiteShare	28147	0.876	0.150	0.024	1	0.79***
ChildShare	28147	0.270	0.034	0.122	0.460	0.25***
Ruralness	28147	4.526	2.919	0	9	2.29***
Humidity	28147	56.781	12.200	14	80	59.36
Topography	28147	7.706	6.209	1	21	7.67***
Plains	28147	0.603	0.486	0	1	0.61
WaterShare	28147	4.874	11.465	0	75	11.91***
WaterTopo	28147	27.956	71.913	0	1200	44.13***
WetPlains	28147	35.532	29.435	0	80	40.08***
WetTopo	28147	418.173	352.102	28	1580	384.91
Floodrisk	28147	87.194	12.753	19	99	91.02***

Note: [a]This column contains the mean values of the independent variables for communities participating in the CRS.

significant relationship between payroll and CRS participation. The result also shows a significant, but negative relationship between property tax revenue and CRS participation. Capital outlay is not a significant predictor of CRS participation.

Flood risk factors in a community are significant determinants of CRS participation. Measures from the Economic Research Service's (ERS) Natural Amenities Index which capture climate and topography, and their interaction, play some role. Specifically, the percent of community area covered by water and humidity both significantly increase CRS participation. As expected, interaction terms (highly variable topography and extensive surface water, highly variable topography and more humidity) are negative and significant determinants of CRS participation as communities are less likely to participate in the CRS in steeper or mountainous topography. More water and flatter topography is typically associated with floodplains and more flooding risk, and the results for the interaction terms in Table 5 are consistent with the notion that greater flood risk is associated with CRS participation. Finally, conditional on those basic correlates of flood risk, peak flood risk in the area is also a positive significant determinant of CRS participation.[1] That basic, county-level climate and topography factors play a significant role even after directly controlling for flooding risk suggests other environmental conditions beyond technical flood risk measures can influence community mitigation.

Two out of the three socio-demographic factors are significant predictors of CRS participation. Share of population that is White and the share of population under the age of 18, both significantly decrease CRS participation. Share of population with a college degree is not a significant predictor of CRS participation.

Table 5. Logistic regression results.

Models	Logistic Regression Coefficient Variables (Robust Std. Err.)
Variables	
ln(payroll)	0.680 ***
	(0.021)
PropTax	−8.33e-06***
	(2.92e-06)
FlowCapital	0.0000133
	(9.25e-06)
HousingValue	0.934***
	(0.202)
HHincome	− 3.123***
	(0.394)
YearBuilt	0.014***
	(0.005)
RentShare	−4.634***
	(0.789)
StayShare	−4.641***
	(0.799)
CollegeShare	1.651
	(1.033)
noHSshare	−7.126***
	(1.042)
WhiteShare	−1.737***
	(0.417)
ChildShare	−3.976***
	(1.324)
Ruralness	−0.051**
	(0.023)
Humidity	0.023*
	(0.012)
Topography	0.145***
	(0.040)
WaterShare	0.032***
	(0.004)
Plains	−1.067***
	(0.717)
WaterTopo	−0.005***
	(0.001)
WetPlains	0.026**
	(0.012)
WetTopo	−0.002***
	(0.001)
Floodrisk	0.011***
	(0.004)
Constant	−10.919
	(11.068)
Observations	**28,140**

Note: ***$p < 0.01$, **$p < 0.05$, *$p < 0.1$.

Political-economy factors are significant predictors of CRS participation. Housing values are significant positive predictors of CRS participation, consistent with greater private gains to homeowners from discounted flood insurance. The share of housing units that are rentals significantly decreases CRS participation, as would be expected if renters apply less pressure on community flood risk managers. Conversely, household income and share of residents not relocating significantly decrease CRS participation rates.

We employed a tobit regression (reported in Table 6) to determine the factors that predict the credits or scores that communities get conditional on participating in the CRS program. Because we cannot interpret the tobit coefficients as effect sizes for actual CRS scores, we focus on the significance and direction of the coefficients. The tobit result suggests positive and significant association between CRS scores and payroll, capital outlay on related categories, housing values, educational attainment, humidity, topography, the percent of a community area covered by water, the interaction between humidity and plains, and community flood risk. The tobit results also show a negative and significant association between CRS scores and amount of property tax, household income, share of renters and share of residents not relocating, share of population not finishing high school, share of a community's population that is White, share of population under the age of 18, and ruralness. In addition, plains, the interaction between the percent of a community area covered by water and topography, and the interaction between humidity and topography, all decrease CRS scores.

We employ a Cragg model, which relaxes some tobit assumptions, to better understand whether the factors that motivate communities to participate in the CRS are the same factors that determine the CRS scores for communities. The Cragg model results indicate that the factors that influence communities' decision to participate in the CRS do not operate similarly in influencing communities' CRS scores. The predictors of CRS participation are indeed different than those determining the intensity of participation. Payroll, household income, share of renters, share of population not finishing high school, share of population that is White, share of population under the age of 18, humidity, topography, plains, percent of community area covered by water, and flood risk are significant determinants of CRS participation but are not significant predictors of CRS score. Additionally, all three interaction terms that significantly predict CRS participation – the percent of a community area covered by water and topography, humidity and plains, and humidity and topography – are not significant predictor of CRS score.

5. Discussion

The size of the government staff does appear to be positively associated with government capacity to participate in the CRS program, but property tax revenues do not also work in this way. Capital outlay on flood-related infrastructure categories, conversely, is positively associated with CRS participation (in the tobit and craggit models) and likely reflects local capacity or interest in flood risk management. We expect higher property tax revenues to lead to more participation in the CRS. Contrary to our expectations, the results from each model indicate a negative and significant relationship between property tax revenue and CRS participation. This finding is at odds with Landry and Li (2012) finding of a positive relationship between CRS participation and property tax revenue. One possible explanation for this negative relationship is that many places' inability to collect property taxes biases its effects in this sample (unlike Landry and Li (2012), who only analyze counties). Another explanation is that, conditional on payroll and housing values, property tax revenues may better capture the effect of higher tax rates. Finally, it might be that the

Table 6. Tobit regression and Cragg's double hurdle results.

Models Variables	Tobit Regression Coefficient (Std. Err.)	Cragg Double Hurdle Coefficient (Std. Err.)	
		Participation	Score
ln(payroll)	713.972***	0.331***	17.981
	(25.365)	(0.010)	(11.240)
PropTax	−0.0113***	−4.72e-06***	-0.006***
	(0.003)	(1.26e-06)	(0.001)
FlowCapital	0.0263***	0.0000105***	0.0202***
	(0.007)	(3.46e-06)	(0.003)
HousingValue	908.905***	0.440***	−223.871**
	(200.014)	(0.094)	(99.463)
HHincome	−3180.822***	−1.512***	28.269
	(430.569)	(.201)	(216.681)
YearBuilt	8.917***	0.005***	−0.988
	(3.341)	(0.002)	(1.480)
RentShare	−5298.117***	−2.416***	−601.757
	(822.932)	(0.385)	(419.568)
StayShare	−5746.344***	−2.54***	−1051.359**
	(818.210)	(0.380)	(436.063)
CollegeShare	2491.044**	0.937*	1091.935**
	(1114.827)	(0.529)	(540.595)
noHSshare	−6894.933***	−3.386***	−337.131
	(1164.905)	(0.542)	(648.052)
WhiteShare	−1663.979***	−0.755*** (0.216)	−151.530 (256.007)
	(463.056)		
ChildShare	−3518.382**	−1.929*** (0.686)	−902.743 (630.078)
	(1420.085)		
Ruralness	−60.716**	−0.022** (0.011)	−50.417*** (11.732)
	(23.642)		
Humidity	25.012**	0.0127** (0.006)	−8.596
	(12.693)		(6.166)
Topography	162.558***	0.0763*** (0.020)	1.330
	(41.302)		(19.278)
WaterShare	32.204***	0.015*** (0.002)	2.229
	(3.657)		(1.653)
Plains	−1273.389*	−0.667*	39.230 (328.808)
	(716.677)	(0.341)	
WaterTopo	−4.289***	−0.002*** (0.000313)	−0.189
	(0.665)		(0.271)
WetPlains	31.466**	0.0151**	5.824
	(12.397)	(0.006)	(5.912)
WetTopo	−2.308***	−0.001*** (.000346)	0.231
	(0.734)		(0.352)
Floodrisk	11.645***	0.005*** (0.002)	1.881
	(4.010)		(1.969)
Constant	−1524.012	−2.192 (3.507)	6446.719 (3210.868)
	(7327.397)		
Observations	**28,140**	**28,140**	**28,140**

Note: ***p < 0.01, **p < 0.05, *p < 0.1.

property tax revenue effect may be proxying for larger communities. Alternative constructions of the property tax variable merit investigations, including a per-household measure (which would better align with Landry and Li's usage) and one that addressed potential nonlinearities (where logging is not an option because, unlike Landry and Li (2012) who study North Carolina counties, many places report $0 in property tax receipts). Unlike an analysis for counties, property tax receipts are not as good a candidate for measuring capacity to participate in the CRS as the size of the government's payroll and its capital outlays for water- and sewerage-related infrastructure. That latter, in particular, is a strong and consistent predictor of both participation in the CRS and attainment of higher CRS scores. In sum, the negative sign on the coefficient of property tax does not support H1, but the significant and positive sign on the coefficients for payroll and *FlowCapital* does support H1.

With regard to flood risk factors, the positive signs on the coefficients of these three variables – percent of community area covered by water, topography, and humidity – indicate support for H2. In other words, communities with higher flood risks are more likely to participate in the CRS. A higher percentage of water coverage indicates a higher likelihood of flooding. More humidity, especially in flatter topography, is a strong predictor of participation. These findings are generally consistent with the expectation that combining water flows with flat areas leads to more flooding. That climate and topography measures matter so much in this model is particularly interesting in light of the control for a more technical 'flood risk' measure. This result is in line with previous research (Landry & Li, 2012) and an important finding to policy makers because it suggests that flood hazard mitigation measures are implemented by communities that are prone to flooding (Landry & Li, 2012). It is also important to recognize that communities appear to be influenced by natural characteristics of their environments beyond what technical flood risk metrics capture.

More than government capacity and natural risk drive CRS participation, however. The results also present evidence in support of H3 and H4. Socio-demographic factors like racial composition, education levels, and age profiles play important roles in explaining CRS participation. Furthermore, political and economic variables explain a great deal of the variation in CRS participation, although not always as expected. Specifically, household income is a significant negative predictor of CRS participation – communities with higher household incomes are less likely than communities with lower household incomes to participate in the CRS. One explanation is that residents of wealthier places are better able to invest in personal flood mitigation measures and may not see the need to demand that their communities participate in the CRS. An alternative explanation is that measures of average income for the region may not be the appropriate income metric and may even be inversely related to the relevant group's income. Income variability among suburban communities appears to play an important role here.

Just as flood risk positively predicting CRS participation is taken to indicate some validity to the overall results, the positive relationship between property values and CRS participation is vital to a political economy approach to understanding the CRS. (As flood insurance premiums are proportional to housing value, the benefits from the CRS discounting rise in property values.) Similarly, a greater share of renters is seen to deter participation, something consistent with a Home Voter hypothesis (Fischel, 2001). Newer housing construction and high turnover rates among residents predicts greater and more intense participation in the CRS, suggesting that expanding (and perhaps sprawling) communities are most apt to see value in the CRS. New homes and recent sales fall under the NFIP purview, making them more likely to have mandatory flood insurance and thus raising the value of CRS participation to communities with more of those residents. Interestingly, these factors associated with private gains to homeowners predict CRS participation but appear unrelated to CRS scores attained. Higher housing values, surprisingly, predict lower CRS scores (and thus lower insurance premium discounts) conditional upon participating at all. The negative role of wealth, even conditional on all the other controls like housing value and education levels, still presents some anomalous results.

It is interesting to note that the factors that motivate communities to participate in the CRS program are generally not the same factors that determine what CRS scores communities that participate in the CRS get. For example, flood risk is a significant predictor of CRS participation but is not a significant predictor of the CRS scores attained by communities. Further, greater property values appear to reduce CRS score achievement rather than increase it. The communities that score highest in the CRS program are a special kind of participating communities, that much is clear. Knowing the specific predictors for CRS participation and CRS scores would be useful to policy makers – it might enable them to develop policies that would incentivize communities who are already participating in the CRS to attain higher CRS scores. Such incentives should target flood reducing measures that would contribute immensely to reducing community vulnerability to flooding.

6. Conclusion

The US suffers huge losses from flooding, both in terms of lives lost and property damage, every year (Gopalakrishnan, 2013). The recognition of persistent losses and the absence of private flood insurance prompted the US federal government to establish the NFIP in 1968. In 1990, the US federal government established, as part of the NFIP, the Community Ratings System, which is a voluntary program aimed at reducing community flood losses and making communities more resilient to flood disasters. Previous research into the factors motivating participation in the CRS typically looked only at single state case studies and did not assess the 'intensity' of participation as measured by the CRS scores. We use national data to understand the factors that motivate communities to participate in the CRS. In addition, we examined the factors that predict a first stage of CRS participation and a second stage of CRS scores using several approaches. The results indicate that local capacity, flood risk factors, socio-demographic characteristics, and political and economic factors are significant predictors of CRS participation. In addition, the results indicate that the factors that motivate communities to participate in the CRS are not the same factors that predict CRS scores.

This national level analysis offers an opportunity to generalize our findings; something that has not been done enough by previous studies. Nevertheless, there are some limitations of the current study. First, there are some independent variables that previous studies argue are important predictors of CRS participation that are not in our study. For instance, flood experience and percentage of senior citizens (Landry & Li, 2012), population density, reduction per policy holder, and flood property damage (Brody et al., 2009). Second, using total CRS score as our dependent variable does not allow us to see the predictor for each of the four groups of scoring activities (i.e., Series 300, 400, 500, and 600). Finally, our models characterize the participation decisions in a cross-sectional setting; it does not model the dynamics of when communities opt to participate or drop out of the CRS program. Assessing these changes over time remains the focus of future research, especially in light of new local flood risk information.

Despite these limitations, this study contributes to the literature on the NFIP and CRS in particular and natural hazard risk reduction in general. We urge researchers to take this national level study a step further by exploring some additional hypotheses about local flood risk map changes, social capital and political activism, and learning from neighboring communities. In addition, decomposing total CRS scores to determine whether different factors motivate communities to focus on some types of activities more than others, can shed light on program efficacy, as well as feasibility of alternative risk management strategies. For example, it would be interesting to know whether high flood-risk communities focus on Series 300 (informational items) more than Series 500 (mostly structural measures).

The results of this study shine light on the drivers that motivate public authorities to engage in community risk management for flooding. This is especially important as flood risks and flood induced losses continue to rise. As one of the criticisms of the NFIP is that it subsidizes building in floodplains (Goodwin, 2013) and thus exacerbates these losses. The CRS program is especially fascinating as it encourages voluntary community-scale flood risk management by further discounting the flood insurance premiums. With most CRS points earned for informational activities or those that do not actually reduce flood risks, that higher-risk communities tend to participate in the CRS and enjoy discounted premiums raises important questions about the sustainability and efficiency of the program. Understanding how to better promote community-wide risk management and public mitigation efforts remains a major policy challenge for natural disaster risks in general (Gopalakrishnan, 2013). It is our hope that this study will help to galvanize support for increased attention to water disasters as well as spur interest in empirical research to inform water policy to make communities more resilient to water disasters.

Note

1. As an important aside, given that flood risk (measured at the 1 km × 1 km grid cell scale) often varies widely within a community, it is interesting to note that the 'max-mean' function performed most consistently in the model runs. The grid cell risks can be aggregated to a block-group level (e.g., mean risk, maximum risk) and those neighborhood level risk indicators can be aggregated up to a county level. Taking the highest value among neighborhood risk levels, where neighborhood risk is defined as the average risk in that neighborhood, proved a strong fit in these models.

References

Anderson, D. R. (1974). The national flood insurance program. Problems and potential. *The Journal of Risk and Insurance, 41*(4), 579–599. doi:10.2307/251956

Brody, S. D., Kang, J. E., & Bernhardt, S. (2010). Identifying factors influencing flood mitigation at the local level in Texas and Florida: The role of organizational capacity. *Natural Hazards, 52*(1), 167–184. doi:10.1007/s11069-009-9364-5

Brody, S. D., Zahran, S., Highfield, W. E., Bernhardt, S. P., & Vedlitz, A. (2009). Policy learning for flood mitigation: A longitudinal assessment of the community rating system in Florida. *Risk Analysis, 29*(6), 912–929. doi: 10.1111/j.1539-6924.2009.01210.x

Browne, M. J., & Hoyt, R. E. (2000). The demand for flood insurance: Empirical evidence. *Journal of Risk & Uncertainty, 20*(3), 291–306. doi:10.1023/A:1007823631497

Cragg, J. G. (1971). Some statistical models for limited dependent variables with application to the demand for durable goods. *Econometrica, 39*(5), 829–844. doi:10.2307/1909582

Dahlhamer, J. M., & D'Souza, M. J. (1997). Determinants of business disaster preparedness in two U.S. metropolitan areas. *International Journal of Mass Emergencies and Disasters, 15,* 265–281.

Federal Emergency Management Agency. (2002). National Flood Insurance Program: Program description. Retrieved from https://s3-us-gov-west-1.amazonaws.com/dam-production/uploads/20130726-1447-20490-2156/nfipdescrip_1_.pdf

Federal Emergency Management Agency. (2011). National Flood Insurance Program: Answers to questions about NFIP. Retrieved from http://www.fema.gov/media-library-data/20130726-1438-20490-1905/f084_atq_11aug11.pdf

Federal Emergency Management Agency. (2013). Community Rating System: About CRS. Retrieved from http://www.floodsmart.gov/floodsmart/pages/crs/community_rating_system.jsp

Fischel, W. A. (2001). *The homevoter hypothesis: How home values influence local government taxation, school finance, and land-use policies.* Cambridge, MA: Harvard Univ Press.

Goodwin, L. (2013, October 22). Many Sandy victims hit with steep flood insurance bills. *Yahoo News.* Retrieved from http://news.yahoo.com/many-sandy-victims-hit-with-steep-flood-insurance-bills-144726355.html

Gopalakrishnan, C. (2013). Water and disasters: A review and analysis of policy aspects. *International Journal of Water Resources Development, 29*(2), 250–271. doi:10.1080/07900627.2012.756133

King, R. O. (2013). *The National Flood Insurance Program: Status and remaining issues for congress* (Congressional Research Service Report R42850). Retrieved from http://www.fas.org/sgp/crs/misc/R42850.pdf

Kousky, C., & Kunreuther, H. (2013). *Addressing affordability in the National Flood Insurance Program* (Resources for the Future Issue Brief 13–02). Retrieved from http://www.rff.org/RFF/Documents/RFF-IB-13-02.pdf

Kousky, C., Olmstead, S., Walls, M., Stern, A., & Macauley, M. (2011). *The role of land use in adaptation to increased precipitation and flooding: A case study in Wisconsin's lower Fox River Basin* (Resources for the Future Report November 2011). Retrieved from http://www.rff.org/RFF/Documents/RFF-Rpt-Kousky%20etal%20GreatLakes%20(2).pdf

Kunreuther, H. (1996). Mitigating disaster losses through insurance. *Journal of Risk and Uncertainty, 12,* 171–187. doi: 10.1007/BF00055792.

Kunreuther, H. & Roth, R. J. (Eds.). (1998). *Paying the price: The status and role of insurance against natural disasters in the United States.* Washington, DC: Joseph Henry.

Landry, C. E., & Li, J. (2012). Participation in the community rating system of NFIP: Empirical analysis of North Carolina counties. *Natural Hazards Review, 13,* 205–220. doi:10.1061/(ASCE)NH.1527-6996.0000073

Landry, C.E., & Jahan-Parvar, M. R. (2011). Flood insurance coverage in the coastal zone. *Journal of Risk and Insurance, 78*(2), 361–388. doi:10.1111/j.1539-6975.2010.01380.x

Ludy, J., & Kondolf, G. M. (2012). Flood risk perception in lands "protected" by 100-year levees. *Natural Hazards, 61*(2), 829–842. doi: 10.1007/s11069-011-0072-6

May, P. J., & Birkland, T. A. (1994). Earthquake risk reduction: An examination of local regulatory efforts. *Environmental Management, 18,* 923–937. doi: 10.1007/BF02393621.

Meyer-Emerick, N., & Momen, M. (2003). Continuity planning for nonprofits. *Nonprofit Management and Leadership, 14,* 67–77. doi: 10.1002/nml.21.

Mileti, D. S. (1999). *Disasters by design: A reassessment of natural hazards in the United States.* Washington, DC: Joseph Henry Press.

Mileti, D. S., Darlington, J. D., Fitzpatrick, C., & O'Brien, P. W. (1993). *Communicating earthquake risk: Societal response to revised probabilities in the Bay Area.* Fort Collins, CO: Hazard Assess Lab and Department of Sociology, Colorado State University.

National Association of Insurance Commissioners. (2012). Biggert-Waters flood insurance reform and modernization act of 2012. Retrieved from http://www.naic.org/documents/cipr_overview_2012_flood_reauthorization.pdf

National Weather Service. (2013). United States flood loss report-water year 2012. Retrieved from http://www.nws.noaa.gov/hic/summaries/WY2012.pdf

Petrolia, D. R., Landry, C. E., & Coble, K. H. (2013). Risk preferences, risk perceptions, and flood insurance. *Land Economics, 89*(2), 227–245.

Posey, J. (2009). The determinants of vulnerability and adaptive capacity at the municipal level: Evidence from floodplain management programs in the United States. *Global environmental change, 19,* 482–493. doi:10.1016/j.gloenvcha.2009.06.003

Sadiq, A.-A. (2010). Digging through disaster rubble in search of the determinants of organizational mitigation and preparedness. *Risk, Hazards & Crisis in Public Policy, 1*(2), 33–62. doi: 10.2202/1944-4079.1005

Stellin, S. (2012, November 8). Reconsidering flood insurance. *The New York Times*, Retrieved from http://www.nytimes.com

Thomas, A., & Leichenko, R. (2011). Adaptation through insurance: Lessons from the NFIP. *International Journal of Climate Change Strategies and Management, 3*(3), 250–263. doi:10.1108/17568691111153401

United States Census Bureau. (1990). *Place list*. Retrieved from http://www.census.gov/geo/reference/docs/codes/PLACElist.txt

United States Department of Transportation. (1996). *Natural disaster study: National pipeline risk index technical report (Task 2)*. Retrieved from https://www.npms.phmsa.dot.gov/data/data_natdis.htm

United States General Accounting Office. (1983). *National Flood Insurance Program: Major changes needed if it is to operate without a federal subsidy* (Report by the Comptroller General of the United States). Retrieved from http://www.gao.gov/assets/140/139341.pdf

Williams, D. T., Carreon, S., & Bradley, J. B. (1992). Evaluation of erosion potential at pipeline crossings. In M. Jennings & N. G. Bhowmik (Eds.), *Hydraulic engineering* (pp. 689–694). New York, NY: American Society of Civil Engineers.

Wooldridge, J. M. (2002). *Econometric analysis of cross-section and panel data*. Cambridge, MA: MIT Press.

Zahran, S., Brody, S. D., Highfield, W. E., & Vedlitz, A. (2010). Non-linear incentives, plan design, and flood mitigation: The case of the federal emergency management agency's community rating system. *Journal of Environmental Planning and Management, 53*(2), 219–239. doi:10.1080/09640560903529410

Zahran, S., Weiler, S., Brody, S. D., Lindell, M. K., & Highfield, W. E. (2009). Modeling national flood insurance policy holding at the county scale in florida, 1999–2005. *Ecological Economics, 68*(10), 2627–2636. doi:10.1016/j.ecolecon.2009.04.021

A historical examination of the Corps of Engineers and natural valley storage protection: the economics and politics of 'green' flood control

Carolyn Kousky

Resources for the Future, Washington, DC, USA

Between 1972 and 1994, the US Army Corps of Engineers undertook five studies in New England evaluating the benefits and costs of protecting natural valley storage (NVS) areas—natural reservoirs—for flood mitigation. Only along the Charles River did benefits outweigh costs. Analysis of the studies finds that the costs of large-scale land acquisition will often exceed the sole benefits of avoided flood damages. To generate net benefits, there must be significant amounts of NVS lands still undeveloped, development pressure on those lands, and downstream areas that would sustain large damages. The NVS studies also raised questions of whether the Corps should be involved in land acquisition, and whether regulating land use could substitute for purchasing land. Note, these findings do not apply to other forms of natural flood-risk reduction, such as levee setbacks, green infrastructure for stormwater management, and multi-purpose projects, which have different economic and institutional contexts.

1. Introduction

There has been growing interest in 'green' approaches to flood-risk management, whereby structural measures are eschewed in favor of some type of floodplain conservation. This has taken a number of forms around the world. One approach is the protection of what the New England Division of the US Army Corps of Engineers has referred to as 'natural valley storage' (NVS). NVS areas are lands, often wetlands, which temporarily store floodwaters, acting as natural reservoirs. While the Corps has been involved in most large investments in structural flood control in the United States, it has a limited history with NVS protection. In the 1970s, it acquired roughly 8500 acres of NVS lands along the Charles River and its tributaries in Massachusetts to protect against increases in flooding. After the approval of this project, the Corps evaluated the benefits and costs of NVS projects in four other New England watersheds between 1972 and 1994. In none of these other cases was an NVS approach found to merit federal investment.

This paper examines in detail these five cases reviewed by the New England Division of the Corps of Engineers to ascertain what made NVS protection economically and institutionally attractive in the Charles River case but not in the other watersheds. Analysis of these studies and supporting documents demonstrates many ways in which the Charles River case was unique. While some findings are historical, in that they are no longer applicable to today's conditions or current Corps study procedures, the analysis does uncover several lessons that can inform today's efforts of floodplain conservation for flood control. These should extend beyond the Corps to the growing number of public and private entities pursuing natural flood-risk management, and not just within the United States, but also in other places around the world. It may also shed insight on why other types of natural flood risk management, such as targeted buyouts or levee setbacks appear to be more popular or feasible than large-scale protection of NVS lands.

The first key finding of the analysis is that large-scale acquisition of land to function as a natural reservoir for the containment of large riverine flood events is unlikely to be economically justified solely by consideration of avoided flood damages downstream. There were three circumstances that led the Corps to conclude there were net benefits for protecting NVS lands in the Charles River case: (1) significant amounts of NVS lands remained undeveloped, (2) those lands faced substantial development pressure such that the counterfactual in the absence of the project was the loss of those lands, and (3) downstream areas would sustain high levels of damage in the event of a flood. All three of these conditions were not present in the other watersheds studied.

That said, the fact that the Charles River NVS project was not replicated elsewhere may have had less to do with economics and more with institutional concerns. The Charles River project raised fundamental questions about whether the Corps – and perhaps the federal government more broadly – should be involved in acquiring large amounts of land for flood control purposes, or whether this type of land acquisition should be the purview of local governments instead. In addition, in the years between approval of the Charles River project and the other Corps studies, both the federal government and states passed legislation providing higher levels of protection to wetlands, thus reducing the likelihood that they would be lost if not purchased. Such regulations were less costly to the government and made land purchases for flood-risk reduction appear redundant.

Note that this paper is focused on analyzing the economic and institutional concerns surrounding the five cases and how they influenced the decision of the Corps to pursue (or not) NVS projects. This paper is not seeking to evaluate ex-post whether any of the assumptions ultimately proved justified or not. It also does not evaluate the hydrologic and hydraulic modeling underlying the studies.

The paper proceeds as follows. The next section provides background on NVS as a flood-risk reduction strategy, information on the Corps and their cost-benefit analysis (CBA), and an overview of each of the five cases. Section 3 then turns to an analysis of the economics of NVS based on the five cases. Section 4 takes up the institutional questions surrounding large-scale land acquisition for flood risk management. Section 5 concludes.

2. Background

2.1. Natural Valley Storage (NVS) for flood-risk reduction

Qualitatively, three different types of flood mitigation strategies for large riverine flood events make use of natural systems.[1] The one discussed in this paper, preserving NVS areas, is explained in more detail in this section. Of note, however, there are two other approaches that would similarly be classified as green strategies for flood-risk reduction: (1) reconnecting rivers to their floodplains through levee setbacks (Opperman et al., 2009); and (2) reducing exposure in floodplains. In the first approach, the channel of the river is widened, giving more room for conveyance of floodwaters. This is done in conjunction with structural measures; that is, levees may be pushed back farther from the river but are still in place to protect development behind them. In the second approach, development is prevented in flood-prone areas or is actively removed once there (such as through federal buyout programs). The goal of this approach is not to alter the hydrology of a system and reduce flood risk downstream, although that might occur, but simply to remove from harm's way structures that could be damaged by floodwaters. The acreage conserved from such buyout programs is substantially less than that envisioned with NVS protection. These approaches have been more commonly employed than NVS protection, and the analysis in this paper may suggest why that is the case. The economic realities and institutional contexts of these approaches are quite different and the conclusions drawn in this paper for NVS do not apply to these other two types of green approaches.

'Natural valley storage' (NVS) is a term that appears to be used almost exclusively by the New England Division of the Corps in the studies reviewed in this paper. These studies use the term to refer to lands in a watershed that can temporarily store floodwaters acting as natural reservoirs – referred to as off-channel storage, and may also move floodwater (New England Division of the Corps of Engineers, 1993). As described in one of the reports for the Charles River project, NVS areas are marshes and swamps that 'modify and desynchronize flood flows in a manner similar to a series of reservoirs' (New England Division of the Corps of Engineers, 1976c, p. 1). NVS areas essentially lag and reduce the flood peak.

The ability of an area to store floodwaters effectively is a function of soil, topography, vegetation, and location in the watershed (New England Division of the Corps of Engineers, 1993). Clay soils do not store floodwaters as effectively as organic matter, for example, and steep slopes do not hold water either. Vegetation slows down flood-waters. Finally, note that natural storage is more effective for floods that peak and recede quickly (New England Division of the Corps of Engineers, 1990, 1993). For floods of a long duration, storage areas will fill and then fail to provide additional storage benefit. This feature impacts the economics of NVS as a flood damage reduction strategy, and is discussed more below.

2.2. *The Corps and cost-benefit analysis*

The Corps' work building flood control projects in the United States goes back to the early twentieth century on the Sacramento and Mississippi Rivers. In 1936, Congress passed the Flood Control Act, which stated that flood control is a proper activity of the federal government. This act also mandated that the benefits of Corps projects outweigh the costs and that the localities benefiting from the project bear a small portion of the total costs. Initially, the Corps undertook only so-called single-purpose projects, which were authorized and constructed for a single reason, such as flood damage reduction. With the passage of legislation in 1944 authorizing several multipurpose dams, this began to change. Multipurpose projects include the provision of other benefits, such as recreation or conservation, for instance, and the Corps has since undertaken many such projects.

Carter and Stern (2011) describe the process of Corps projects from start to finish. Flood control projects begin with a local sponsor requesting Corps involvement. Congress then authorizes a reconnaissance study to gauge federal interest in a project and the extent of support among possible nonfederal sponsors. If the project is favorably reported, then the Corps conducts a feasibility study on the project. The feasibility study formulates solutions to the problem and evaluates them, with an engineering analysis and a CBA as well as a review of environmental impacts pursuant to the National Environmental Policy Act of 1969. When a particular project is recommended, Congress must then authorize and appropriate funds for construction of the project. In 1986, Congress passed legislation that updated certain Corps practices. Of note, the cost sharing by local sponsors was increased from 25% to 35%, and the local partner was directed to share in the costs of the planning stages.

The Corps has been directed by Congress to consider projects in the national interest. Thus, Corps CBAs evaluate benefits and costs to the country as a whole, not from the more narrow perspective of the locality. Current practice for these studies is found in the 1983 *Economic and Environmental Principles and Guidelines for Water and Related Land Resources Implementation Studies* and related Corps guidance documents. The Corps is to choose a project that maximizes 'national economic development', or the economic value of the national output of goods and services, unless there are overriding reasons to do otherwise. Corps studies also calculate impacts on national environmental quality. Congress mandated an updating of the *Principles and Guidelines* in 2007, and a final draft revision was released in 2013; these new documents did not apply to any of the cases examined in this paper. The new guidelines are intended to allow communities more flexibility in pursing their own priorities and improve inclusion of environmental benefits in project evaluation. The draft document requires consideration of nonstructural approaches, evaluation of quantifiable and non-quantifiable impacts, and inclusion of a range of environmental, social, and economic impacts.

Historically, the Corps focused primarily on structural flood control measures. In the years covering the studies here, and subsequently, the Corps' mission began to expand to include a greater emphasis on environmental protection and restoration. There has also been a shift at the Corps toward greater interest in non-structural flood control measures (e.g., Galloway, 2005), although not specifically NVS. Water Resource Development Acts passed in 1974, 1986, 1990, 1992, 1996, and 1999 all included provisions toward broader consideration of the environment or nonstructural measures (see Buss, 2005; Galloway, 2005; National Research Council, 1999). These acts, and other changes, including the updating of the Principles and Guidelines and adoption of Environmental Operating Principles in 2002, have altered Corps practice, such that the examination in this paper needs to be viewed purely as a historical examination. That said, there are still lessons to be learned for today's activities in green flood-risk reduction: many of the economic and institutional questions raised by these projects remain. Due to changes in Corps goals and activities, however, this paper attempts to focus on those findings that can be useful to consider in today's environment.

2.3. The New England cases

This paper presents the results of detailed analyses of five different NVS case studies undertaken by the Corps in New England between 1972 and 1994. Some of these reports are reconnaissance studies and some are feasibility studies, so the detail of the analysis varies. In addition, in 1991 the Corps was authorized to undertake a study of NVS in Massachusetts under its Planning Assistance to States Program; this report provides a higher-level discussion of the economics of NVS, including a review of the Charles, Spicket, and Taunton reports, and was thus reviewed along with the specific case documents (New England Division of the Corps of Engineers, 1993). The original studies and all supporting documentation were obtained for each case and were carefully reviewed and examined. In addition, any relevant gray literature on the studies or references that were pertinent to analysis of the studies were obtained and evaluated. The five rivers and the states in which they are located include the following:

(1) Charles River; Massachusetts (reports in 1971, 1972, and 1976)
(2) Connecticut River basin; Connecticut, Massachusetts, New Hampshire, and Vermont (reports in 1974 and 1994)
(3) Neponset River basin; Massachusetts (reports in 1979 and 1982)
(4) Taunton River; Massachusetts (report in 1978)
(5) Spicket River; Massachusetts and New Hampshire (report in 1990)

Figure 1 maps each of these watersheds. As can be seen, most are small, with the exception of the Connecticut Basin. A brief overview of each case is given in this section.

2.3.1. Charles River basin

The Charles River runs 80 miles from Echo Lake to its mouth at Boston Harbor and has a drainage area of 307 square miles. According to the Corps, the basin is divided into three hydrologically dissimilar sub-watersheds (New England Division of the Corps of Engineers, 1976b). The lower basin, where the Charles empties into the harbor, is a highly developed urban area that includes the cities of Boston and Cambridge. The middle and upper sections are more suburban or rural. In 1955, Hurricane Diane spawned a

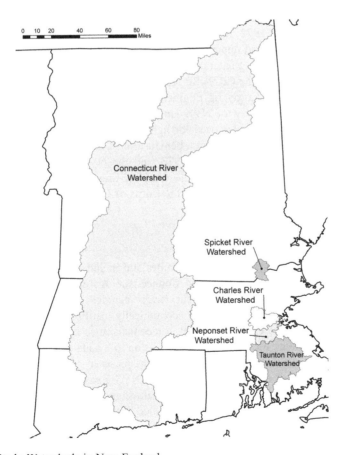

Figure 1.   Study Watersheds in New England.

devastating flood, causing approximately \$5.5 million worth of damage, largely in the lower basin (New England Division of the Corps of Engineers, 1978b). This spurred demand for flood control. In 1965, Congress authorized a feasibility study. In 1968, the New England Division finished the first part of the study, which recommended upgrading of a dam built in 1910 at the mouth of the river. This dam was completed in 1978.

In 1968, another storm caused a flood close to the level of the 1955 flood. The Corps was able to examine the flooding firsthand, finding that in the upper and middle portions of the watershed, the flood crest moved extremely slowly; ultimately, it took a month for all of the stormwater to reach the dam (Chandler & Doyle, 1978). This confirmed the Corps' belief that wetlands were effectively controlling flooding in the middle and upper basins. After examining multiple flood control options for these basins, the Corps ultimately recommended fee simple purchase or conservation easement acquisition of wetlands in the watershed. The recommended project involved the acquisition of wetlands in 16 communities along the Charles and its tributaries that together would 'retard flood flows and act as a reservoir system in retaining and de-synchronizing flood flows' (New England Division of the Corps of Engineers, 1976b, p. 8). Many public meetings were held, including 12 sponsored by a citizen advisory committee that more than 600 people attended (Chandler & Doyle, 1978). In the final 1971 meeting at the completion of the study, the Corps' plan was endorsed unanimously and received support from the US Department of the Interior, the Fish and Wildlife Service, and the governor of Massachusetts (Chandler & Doyle, 1978; New England Division of the Corps of Engineers, 1976c). The 1972 report recommended the Charles River NVS project (CRNVSP) on the middle and upper portions of the watershed.

The next step was obtaining federal authorization, which came in the Water Resources Development Act in 1974. The CRNVSP was the first of its type to be authorized (New England Division of the Corps of Engineers, 1976c). It protected, through federal acquisition, roughly 8500 acres of NVS lands for the flood mitigation benefits those lands provided. The lands are also used for light recreational activities and managed for fish and wildlife. Corps studies suggest a benefit-to-cost ratio of more than 2:1 for these investments. Land acquisition began in 1977, and the NVS project was completed in 1984. It remains the only Corps flood project in New England to use wetlands to reduce flood damages (New England Division of the Corps of Engineers, 1993).[2]

2.3.2. Connecticut River basin

The Connecticut River basin drains 11,250 miles and includes areas of four states: New Hampshire, Vermont, Massachusetts, and Connecticut. An early study of nonstructural flood control options on the Connecticut River included acquisition as part of the strategies examined, but found it was not economically justified (Cheney, 1974).

In 1994, however, the Corps undertook a reconnaissance study at the request of the Connecticut River Valley Flood Control Commission to evaluate the impacts of development on NVS and whether the Corps could help preserve NVS areas (New England Division of the Corps of Engineers, 1994). Seven NVS areas were identified, four along the main stem and three along tributaries. The main stem areas, representing 83% of total storage, were studied in detail. The study evaluated obtaining easements on 22,750 acres of land but did not evaluate structural alternatives. The report found protecting NVS to have a benefit-to-cost ratio of 0.11:0.23, depending on the scenario, and thus it was not recommended (New England Division of the Corps of Engineers, 1994).

2.3.3. Neponset River basin

The Neponset River has its headwaters in Foxborough, Massachusetts; from there it flows toward Boston Harbor, forming the southern boundary of the city. It drains roughly 115 square miles and is bordered to the north by the Charles River basin. In 1979, the Corps undertook a reconnaissance study for the Neponset River basin, which recommended further analysis in a second phase of both structural and nonstructural alternatives, with an emphasis on NVS (New England Division of the Corps of Engineers, 1979). The reconnaissance study identified a large amount of existing wetlands in the basin and expressed concern that their development could increase flood damages.

The phase II study examined three potential alternatives: structural local protection; a combination of floodproofing, elevation of some properties, and an early warning system; and protection of NVS areas. The study concluded that preserving the NVS lands would ensure the most widespread protection, but that it should be done through zoning and existing legislation. An extensive program of land acquisition was considered to be 'prohibitively costly and unnecessary' (New England Division of the Corps of Engineers, 1982). Since regulations were deemed to be sufficient to protect the land, the Corps did not evaluate land easements or acquisition in detail.

2.3.4. Taunton River

The Taunton River basin lies just south of the Neponset basin. It drains 570 square miles, primarily in southeastern Massachusetts. The Corps completed a study of the basin in 1978. The report evaluated several alternatives but concluded that there was no federal role in the basin. It did stress, however, that existing regulations should be used to protect NVS areas. The study noted that the basin was not highly developed at the time, which is part of the reason why it had not had major flood problems, but that residential and industrial development pressures were growing (New England Division of the Corps of Engineers, 1978a).

2.3.5. Spicket River

The Spicket River, a tributary of the Merrimack River, is located in northwestern Massachusetts and southern New Hampshire. It is roughly 15 miles long, draining 78 square miles. In 1990, the Corps completed a general investigation study for the basin (New England Division of the Corps of Engineers, 1990). The investigation was spurred by serious flooding in 1987, which generated interest in the development of a flood loss reduction plan. The study examined several flood reduction options, including one that would minimize the loss of NVS. The Spicket River had sizable NVS areas at the time of the study, roughly 2220 acres, two-thirds of which were located in Salem, New Hampshire and Methuen, Massachusetts. The study found that a flood warning system would generate net benefits, but protection of NVS lands would not.

3. The benefits and costs of NVS

In four of the five case studies, setting aside significant amounts of land to manage large riverine flood events was not economically justified by the sole benefits of avoided flood damages (with no consideration of any co-benefits). To control a hundred-year flood event, a substantial amount of land is required, generating high costs. Exactly how much land varies by watershed size, typography, and conditions, but is much larger than the amount needed to contain stormwater, for example, or when simply buying out a few flood-prone structures. EPA provides a rough estimate that a one-acre wetland can store around three-acre feet of water (Environmental Protection Agency [EPA], 2006). In addition, because wetlands drain slowly, their full storage potential may not be available during any given storm event; this is especially important for large, regional floods of long duration (Potter, 1994). For this reason, wetlands are most likely to be effective in mitigating the effects of smaller floods and may not substantially attenuate peaks for very large flood events. That said, at least one study has found that flood attenuation increases as wetland area in the watershed increases, but that wetland areas covering only a small percentage of the watershed can still provide substantial reductions in peak flows (De Laney, 1995). That study, however, did not address whether the costs of conserving that land were outweighed by the avoided flood damages.

Section 3.1 provides an overview of how the potential NVS investments were evaluated in the CBAs of the five studies. Section 3.2 then turns to three key reasons NVS protection was found to generate net benefits in the Charles River case.

3.1. Overview of the Corps CBAs

Corps CBAs for flood damage reduction projects compare the benefits of a project – measured as avoided flood damages – with its full costs. The studies compare 'with-project' conditions to 'without-project' conditions. The benefits of the projects are thus defined as the difference between flood damages with the project and flood damages without the project. All benefits and costs are reported and compared in annual terms. Benefits accrue through the useful life of the project and are discounted back to present values. Most flood control projects use a project life of 50–100 years. For the CRNVSP, the Corps assumed a useful life of 100 years and used a discount rate of 6⅛% (New England Division of the Corps of Engineers, 1976b). This is similar to the Taunton study, which assumed 100 years and used a 6⅝% rate (New England Division of the Corps of Engineers, 1978a). Both of the Connecticut River studies assumed 50 years; they differed in the discount rate, with one using 5⅞% and the other using 8% (Cheney, 1974; New England Division of the Corps of Engineers, 1994). The discount rate is clearly critical in determining how great a weight future benefits play in the overall net benefit calculation. Much has been written on the Corps practice and choice of a discount rate (see, for example, Powers, 2003), and that discussion is not rehashed here.

Benefit estimations for flood control projects are based on guidelines from the US Water Resources Council. An overview of this process is provided by the New England Division of the Corps of Engineers (1993). First, a study area is defined, which is, at a minimum, the 100-year floodplain. Structures in the study area are catalogued. Elevations are determined for all structures so that damages can be estimated for multiple flood heights, or stages. Stage-damage functions are used to relate flood stage levels to dollars of damage. The stage-damage function is coupled with a hydrologic and hydraulic analysis that estimates stage-frequency curves that relate stages to probability of occurrence for both with- and without-project conditions. Coupling these functions gives a damage-frequency curve, which can be used to derive estimates of expected annual damages. Annual benefits are estimated as the difference between the expected annual damages with and without the project.

Three things play a role in determining the flood damage reduction benefits of NVS protection:

(1) projected development of NVS areas in the without-project condition;

(2) the effect of storage areas on flood levels; and

(3) the relationship between flood levels and flood damage.

We return to (1) in Section 3.2 below. Corps hydrologic modeling determines (2); this is not a focus of this paper and is not analyzed here. The outcome of (3) is based on the chosen depth-damage curve – a stair-step function by foot of water depth that calculates damage as a percentage of building value for each depth level. Such functions are developed for groups of structures that are likely to face similar damage, such as two-story residential units that have a basement. Preferably, depth-damage functions should be used that are specific to a given locality, are based on the specific type of structure, and have been validated against past damage. Such curves are rarely available, however, and national averages are often applied. The difference in damage estimations across depth-damage functions can be quite large (see, for example, Merz, Kreibich, Thieken, & Schmidtke, 2004), but none of the studies included any sensitivity analysis on this. Depth-damage functions remain today partially 'art' without solid validation in most locations.

The costs of a project include all expenditures to build and operate the project. For NVS studies, the vast majority of the costs are for property acquisition through fee simple purchase or purchase of easements. Other costs include those associated with land acquisition (e.g., mapping, surveying, appraisals, negotiations, legal costs, title costs, as well as recording and transfer fees). Since a large amount of land is required, these costs can be quite high. For instance, in the Charles River case, 8500 acres were preserved, and in the Connecticut River case it was estimated that easements would be needed on 22,750 acres of land. In all studies reviewed here, the costs of purchasing land were calculated at market value. For the Charles River study, the market value was estimated using comparable sales, appraisals, and assessments. For both the Taunton and Spicket River studies, a per-acre estimated value was calculated and used with little justification. The 1993 report compared the average per-acre costs of land acquisition, in constant 1990 dollars, used in several of the studies and found that they were lowest for the Taunton case at $880 and highest for the Spicket River case at $5000; the Charles was in the middle at $2400 (New England Division of the Corps of Engineers, 1993). (Translated to 2013 dollars, these are $1581 per acre for the Taunton study, $8982 per acre for the Spicket study, and $4311 per acre for the Charles study.) Higher land costs can be justified when the benefits are also higher.

While easements lower the costs of using NVS, it is usually impossible to determine a priori which, if any, property owners would choose an easement. For the CRNVSP, the Corps valued all lands for fee simple purchase, stating that this would 'ensure absolute protection', although they did note that, when requested by landowners, they might pursue easements instead (New England Division of the Corps of Engineers, 1976c, p. 4). However, contrary to this reasoning, the Connecticut River analysis assumed that all acquisition would be through easements, as this would provide the same protection at lower cost (New England Division of the Corps of Engineers, 1994). Neither report calculated and compared the costs of all land acquisition being fee simple versus through easements.

3.2. *Achieving net benefits*

The studies varied in the level of detail in their economic analysis – they were different types of Corps studies – and the assumptions made varied across them, as well. While it is not possible to have an apples-to-apples comparison, then, of all costs and benefits under the same set of assumptions, examining the pattern and implications of the various assumptions made in the analyses suggests some overarching findings. These are discussed here. In particular, it appears that three factors combined in the Charles River case to produce avoided flood damages that outweighed costs:[3]

(1) extensive NVS still in existence;
(2) significant development pressure on NVS lands, but still manageable land costs; and
(3) downstream areas that would sustain considerable damage should a flood occur.

In addition, and perhaps even more important, there was not substantial institutional opposition to the Corps engaging in land protection; this issue is discussed further in Section 5. This section discusses the three criteria just listed in more detail.

First, a plan to use NVS for flood mitigation must be pursued before all NVS lands have been lost to development. Although this seems obvious, it is difficult in many watersheds that are already heavily developed. According to the New England Division of the Corps of Engineers (1972), one way in which the Charles River project was 'remarkable' was that it was undertaken 'early enough to implement an optimal solution' (p. i). The Corps found that around 10,000 acres of the watershed had 'superior flood retention capabilities' (p. 52). The 17 areas ultimately chosen for the project were estimated to control 75% of Charles River watershed wetland and lake storage, equivalent to about 42,000 acre-feet.

In other studies, the Corps also found substantial amounts of NVS in existence; this is a necessary but not sufficient condition for justifying an NVS approach. For example, the Corps found that 13% of the Neponset basin was still in wetlands, much of it along the river, where it provided additional capacity in the channel for detention of floodwaters; if lost, this would increase peak flood flows by anywhere from 25% to 70%, depending on the site (New England Division of the Corps of Engineers, 1982). Similarly, the Spicket River basin was found to have substantial amounts of NVS areas still in existence; if these were developed, this could lead to increases in flood damages downstream (New England Division of the Corps of Engineers, 1990). Other factors prevented the Corps from recommending the protection of these areas through land acquisition, discussed below.

The justification for an NVS approach is slightly different from that for structural flood control measures[4] in that NVS is not implemented to reduce today's flood damage, but to prevent an increase in future flood damages. This was stated as the specific design purpose of the CRNVSP: 'communities in the Upper Charles are not now susceptible to destructive flooding but as the watershed becomes developed flood damages will occur' (New England Division of the Corps of Engineers, 1976b, p. 9). Under this framing, the projected loss of storage under the 'without-project' condition becomes critical. Assumptions about future growth and flood damages can drive the economics of NVS.

The assumed rate of development of NVS lands in the absence of their protection varied across the cases and the reports used various arguments to justify the assumptions made. In the main report for the Charles River case, the Corps noted that a 1967 study by the Massachusetts Department of Natural Resources estimated 1% annual wetland loss for the state as a whole, but the Corps estimated a loss rate of more than double that in the upper and middle portions of the Charles River watershed (New England Division of the Corps of Engineers, 1972). The report justified this assumption with references to local conditions: the watershed's location near metropolitan Boston and the construction of two new circumferential interstate highways (New England Division of the Corps of Engineers, 1976b). This led the Corps to assume a 30% loss of storage by 1990. As an example of the development pressure at the time, while the Corps was scoping the Charles River project, it had to drop two of the locations under consideration because development occurred there, reducing them to less than the determined 100-acre minimum size and lessening the floodwater retention capacity. A sensitivity analysis was done on their assumption of wetland loss, with loss ratios of 10%, 20%, and 40% all examined (New England Division of the Corps of Engineers, 1976b). Benefits exceeded costs for down to a 20% loss. The projected loss of 30% by 1990 of NVS areas led to an increase in damages of 34% (New England Division of the Corps of Engineers, 1993).

That said, while this was a high rate of loss, the Corps assumed an even higher rate of 50% loss of wetland areas as the without-project condition in the 1990 Spicket River study. This was a much higher loss than assumed in the CRNVSP; no justification was given for this choice, although the report also examined loss rates of 10%, 20%, 30%, and 40% (New England Division of the Corps of Engineers, 1990). For no scenario were the benefits found to exceed the costs. The lack of net benefits in this case was due to high land values.

In areas of high development pressure, the costs of land will also be higher, making the project more costly. Property values reflect the opportunity cost of the land, or the value of the next best alternative use. When there is development pressure, this will be higher. No study discussed this point: for net benefits the increased benefits from projected land conversion must outweigh the higher land costs. In the Spicket case, with per acre costs of $5000 (1990 dollars), even a 50% loss of NVS lands did not generate net benefits. If, however, land had been valued at the amount in the Charles River case, benefits would have roughly equaled costs, and if the land values had been the same as those in the Taunton study, the project would have generated net benefits.[5] This example shows that while high development pressure is needed to justify NVS acquisition, it is also the case that if this drives up the opportunity costs of land too high, NVS protection will fail to generate net benefits.

The role of other regulations is also important in defining the without-project conditions, because if storage areas are unlikely to be lost, one would have little justification to pay for their protection. In other contexts, this issue has been referred to as 'additionality' – attempting to ensure that conservation payments actually generate conservation that would not have otherwise occurred (e.g., Murray, Sohngen, & Ross, 2007; Wunder 2007). The CRNVSP analysis was done before the adoption of several state and federal laws that were designed to slow the rate of conversion of wetlands. These include the Massachusetts Wetlands Protection Act, regulations promulgated under Section 404 of the Clean Water Act, regulations required by communities participating in the National Flood Insurance Program, and Executive Order 11988. These laws and regulations were invoked in subsequent studies to argue that land acquisition was not needed because, if these laws were enforced, the without-project condition would not see dramatic conversion of NVS lands. This is discussed further in Section 4.

In the 1994 Connecticut River basin study, two scenarios of development, a moderate or existing growth trends scenario and a 'worst-case scenario', were estimated. These were informed by the existing regulations and laws, as well as historical population growth, projections from the various states, employment rates, and current land use. Despite considering the role of regulations, the study projected positive development of NVS lands on a community-by-community basis. The Corps estimated development growth at 5% for most communities, with some communities experiencing rates between

6% and 12%. For communities participating in the National Flood Insurance Program (NFIP), the report assumed that 35% of the undeveloped and unprotected floodway fringe would be developed in areas with floodways mapped by the Federal Emergency Management Agency (FEMA) (development in the floodway is prohibited but can occur in the fringe if the first floor is elevated above the base flood level) and 20% of the entire undeveloped and unprotected 100-year floodplain would be developed in the other communities (New England Division of the Corps of Engineers, 1994).[6] These assumptions follow an often stated belief that the NFIP, while imposing some regulations on development, has actually accelerated development in floodplains by making insurance available. There is not conclusive evidence on this point, although it has been observed the NFIP has generally pushed development up, through elevation requirements, but not out of the floodplain (Platt, Salvesen, & Baldwin, 2002).

The Connecticut River project was determined to be uneconomic because it did not meet the third criterion of areas that would sustain high levels of damage in the event of a flood. The benefits of NVS conservation come not just from the ability of these lands to hold floodwaters, but also from their ability to hold floodwaters that otherwise would have damaged property. The early Connecticut River analysis noted that the downstream population centers were already protected against floods greater than the 100-year event by dikes and floodwalls. For NVS protection to provide benefits, it would need to protect against much rarer flood events, but the use of NVS for such events would require such enormous amounts of land conserved that the costs would far outweigh the benefits (Cheney, 1974). As mentioned earlier, for large floods of long duration, NVS areas can fill and fail to provide additional protection. The report did not discuss whether NVS areas might prevent failure of the structural flood control measures and this possibility generate enough avoided flood damages to warrant containment of higher magnitude flood events. Similarly, for the Neponset River, the Corps determined that loss of NVS in the upper watershed would not have large impacts downstream, because a large downstream area of NVS could absorb any loss of the upstream areas (New England Division of the Corps of Engineers, 1993). As noted in the reconnaissance study, 'Unless most wetland areas in a basin are located upstream of existing or potential damage areas, they have little effectiveness in mitigating floodflow' (New England Division of the Corps of Engineers, 1979, p. 23).

Likewise, in cases that simply have little development to protect from flooding, protecting NVS will not generate high benefits in terms of avoided flood damages. In the Taunton case, for example, little development downstream meant that any impact of protection on damage reduction would be minimal. The report concluded that '[b]asin-wide acquisition of the larger swamps within the basin by the Federal Government is not economically justified due to the relative lack of downstream development and the high potential of flooding due to tidal influence' (New England Division of the Corps of Engineers, 1978a, D-30). The Corps examined two smaller areas for acquisition where the benefits were thought to potentially be the highest. Some of this land was already protected. In the unprotected area considered, the Corps found that, to generate net benefits, protection would have to reduce damages by more than 50%, an amount that was found unlikely given projected future growth and development in the area.

By contrast, the existence of highly populated and developed areas in the Charles River watershed that would experience serious damages in the event of a flood made the NVS project generate much larger benefits. In addition, in the CRNVSP analysis, the Corps assumed future growth in the areas at risk from flooding, as it was a time of increasing development and real income growth; in contrast, the Corps did not make this assumption for the Spicket River analysis, the Connecticut River analysis, or the Neponset

River study (Cheney, 1974; New England Division of the Corps of Engineers, 1993, 1982). In 1993, a report by the Corps noted that the assumptions in the Charles River case were made as a result of 'extreme developmental pressures' at that time, and that '[s]imilar assumptions would be difficult to justify today' (New England Division of the Corps of Engineers, 1993, p. iii). This assumption of increasing damages in the Charles resulted in larger benefits being found for NVS protection.

Additional benefits of land conservation, such as provision of various ecosystem services or use for passive recreation, were not used in any of the studies to justify an NVS approach. In the Charles River case, the Corps did monetize other benefits – fishing, habitat creation, hunting, and nature study – but these were only 16.5% of flood control benefits and the project would have still had a positive benefit to cost ratio even if they were excluded (New England Division of the Corps of Engineers, 1976a). Environmental benefits are now being more widely included in project evaluation across federal agencies.[7] Within the Corps, it has been noted that consideration of ecosystem restoration and recreation benefits has made some green approaches, such as buyouts, more economically feasible (Buss, 2005). As far I am aware, there are no studies evaluating how inclusion of co-benefits could alter the economics of NVS. That said, other approaches to natural flood-risk reduction, such as buyouts and levee setbacks mentioned earlier, are benefiting from a broadened scope that includes additional benefits beyond flood control.[8] When considering buyouts, the Corps can include as benefits the services created by the new land with the structures removed (Shabman & Scodari, 2012). The Corps has also begun considering explicitly multi-benefit projects, such as the Hamilton City Flood Damage Reduction and Ecosystem Restoration project, which included levee setbacks and restoration of habitat, and was designed with both flood protection and restoration as twin goals. Such multi-benefit projects are becoming increasingly popular. This could increase project costs, but also dramatically increase project benefits. And communities certainly value these additional benefits that can increase the quality of life of an area and attract residents. 'Recreation-induced regional economic development', however, was not something that was included in the NVS studies, as it was often considered a transfer from one region to another and Corps analysis takes the point of view of society as a whole (New England Division of the Corps of Engineers, 1993, p. 36).

4. Is the corps a land protection agency?

Following the CRNVSP, two institutional arguments were made that pushed toward a rejection of NVS protection projects by the Corps: (1) existing regulations provide sufficient protection for NVS lands, such that the 'without-project' condition in Corps CBAs should realistically show little conversion of these areas, and (2) even if there is not existing regulatory protection for NVS lands, their protection should not be accomplished through land acquisition by the Corps. The latter argument embeds both the issues of whether land acquisition, as opposed to regulation, is the best tool for protecting NVS lands, and if it is, whether the Corps should be the one to acquire land or whether such protection should be the responsibility of local governments.

Regarding the first argument, following the CRNVSP, many laws were passed that decreased the likelihood that wetlands would be filled, offering greater protection for NVS areas. These included federal regulations, such as Section 404 of the Clean Water Act and regulations required for community participation in the National Flood Insurance Program, as well as state and local regulations. For example, Massachusetts passed the Wetlands Protection Act, which requires review of work that could alter wetlands and other resource areas, including 100-year floodplains, riverfronts, and waterways. In addition, some communities in the studies had adopted local zoning ordinances that provided protection for at least some NVS areas. Consideration of these new protections fundamentally changed what the Corps assumed as the without-project condition. For example, in the study for the Neponset River, the Corps concluded that if existing regulations were enforced, most storage areas would be protected; thus the Corps never even undertook an economic analysis for protecting these areas (New England Division of the Corps of Engineers, 1979, 1993). That said, the Phase II report at one point contradicts this assertion, noting that '[e]xtensive filling of natural storage in wetlands has occurred in the past and is continuing', and that '[c]ommunities throughout the Neponset River Basin do not have the means to implement and enforce this legislation', but then still concludes with a recommendation for stricter enforcement of regulations, not acquisition (New England Division of the Corps of Engineers, 1982, pp. 2–23, 2–29). The report for the Taunton River also noted that existing regulations should do the job (New England Division of the Corps of Engineers, 1978a).

The reports subsequent to the CRNVSP also raised questions on the second point, whether the Corps should be involved in land acquisition. As noted by Shabman (1972, p. 93), the CRNVSP raised the issue of 'whether the Corps ought to be involved at all in just purchasing and holding land, even if this is the only technically sound means of providing flood control'. The CRNVSP had many supporters, as demonstrated by letters written in favor of the project and appended to the main report (New England Division of the Corps of Engineers, 1972). Still, it has been noted that administration officials were concerned at the time about whether flood control authority within the Corps should include land acquisition on a large scale, and this delayed approval of the project (Platt & McMullen, 1979). The Office of Management and Budget also was worried about the burdens such an approach could place on the federal government (Larson & Dingman, 1981). Beyond the widespread public support, one reason the CRNVSP prevailed amid these concerns could have been its nexus with an already constructed Corps project; the Corps found that if many more NVS areas were lost in the watershed, runoff would become so great that it could exceed the flood control abilities of the pumping facilities and dam at the mouth of the Charles (Shabman, 1972). After the CRNVSP, the view appears to have emerged that large-scale land acquisition, particularly if not tied to a structural Corps project, was not the role of the Corps. For example, in the Spicket River basin, the Corps concluded that '[i]mplementation of sound land use measures is, for the most part, a community responsibility' (New England Division of the Corps of Engineers, 1990, p. 19). While there is much written on division of responsibility and federalism related to emergency response (e.g., Landy, 2008), as far as I am aware, this topic has not been analyzed with respect to ex-ante flood risk reduction measures.

Despite the argument that land acquisition and land use regulation is the domain of local governments, the Corps and others have raised several cautionary points about the ability of local governments to effectively constrain development of NVS areas, which could be taken to potentially justify a federal role in NVS protection. In the first main report on the Charles River project, the Corps noted that absent 'external coordination, municipalities will pursue independent development plans, nibbling away at marsh storage areas piecemeal until in the aggregate effect of their expansion is felt as a major flood disaster' (New England Division of the Corps of Engineers, 1972, p. 30). This was echoed by scholars who observed that basins contain multiple jurisdictions, and controlling externalities related to flood risk are challenging and made even more difficult by the low probability of major floods and the spatial separation between land use changes and their impact (Kousky & Zeckhauser, 2006; Platt & McMullen, 1979). The challenges associated with ecological boundaries that do not match political boundaries – as noted here for the case of natural systems for flood-risk reduction – has been a discussion in multiple issues related to watershed management and many ecosystem services more broadly (e.g., Barham, 2001; Heal et al., 2001). Various institutional arrangements have emerged or been proposed in different contexts to address this disconnect, one being federal responsibility.

Removing NVS protection as a Corps activity also creates an apparent inequity in that federal dollars are used to cost-share the construction of structural flood protection through the Corps, but there is no equivalent program to cost-share land acquisition, should a community prefer it (Larson & Dingman, 1981). This inequity arises if one assumes that certain objectives justify federal spending – such as flood risk management, regardless of how that objective is achieved. Another argument, however, is that federal spending can be justified for certain means, like building structural flood control measures, but not others, such as land acquisition, regardless of the ultimate objective.

Some localities may prefer some amount of land acquisition, even if not fully justifiable economically by avoided flood damages because of the myriad other benefits such lands provide, as discussed at the end of Section 3.2. These concerns may be part of the shift that began occurring in this time period and continues today, away from simple NVS protection to Corps projects that unite environmental protection and restoration of floodplains with limited structural flood control and enhancement of riverine recreational activities. Such projects are now under way in several communities, as mentioned below.

5. Conclusion

This paper has examined five cases between 1972 and 1994 where the Corps investigated acquiring NVS lands for the flood damage reduction doing so could provide. While the benefits of this approach was found to outweigh the costs of acquiring land in the Charles River watershed of Massachusetts, that case was unique in many respects. The middle and upper portions of the watershed had much NVS land still undeveloped, and yet pressure to develop this land was arguably strong and growing. This led to the without project condition assuming loss of a substantial portion of lands and also led to an assumption that downstream damages would be getting worse over time – in an already highly developed area where a flood would be quite costly. Later Corps documents noted that the development pressure would have been hard to justify in later years or other locations. Despite the development pressure, land costs were not so high as to make project costs exceed benefits. The other watersheds examined did not share all these characteristics.

The Charles River project was also undertaken before many federal and state regulations were in place, which, if assumed to be enforced, would limit the conversion of wetlands to development over time. The Corps argued in subsequent reports that these regulatory tools should be used to protect NVS lands rather than land purchase by the federal government. This was in part an economic argument: regulation is cheaper and if it is working, there are no additional benefits to conservation. It was also part an institutional argument: land conservation on a large scale is not a responsibility of the Corps. These two issues both served to push the Corps away from replicating the CRNVSP in the years following its approval.

These economic and political challenges surrounding substantial investments in land protection for the sole purpose of avoided flood damages may partially explain the growth in other green approaches to flood-risk reduction and in multi-purpose projects by both the Corps and other agencies and groups. More limited floodplain buyouts or use of green approaches for managing smaller-scale events, such as urban stormwater management, seem to be gaining more traction in recent years, and have different economics (see, e.g., Valderrama et al., 2013). In addition, there is growing interest in projects with multiple purposes that combine floodplain conservation with improvements in recreational opportunities along rivers and a combination of structural and nonstructural flood control measures. The Corps has been involved in several of these projects, such as in Napa, California; along the Truckee River in Nevada; and in Dallas, Texas.[9] These projects are all examples illustrating that, since the cases examined here, the Corps has moved increasingly in the direction of combining more limited land preservation with other flood mitigation strategies, as well as including a larger range of benefits in projects, such as using ecosystem restoration and recreation as benefits of a project (Buss, 2005). Combining all these benefits can help offset the costs of the project.

Detailed analysis of these other types of approaches to natural flood risk management would be useful complementary work (Kousky, 2010). They raise questions of whether the 'national interest' should be redefined in terms of a broader range of benefits, regardless of the main project purpose, and also how to choose projects when the Corps and local stakeholders may not agree on the best approach – particularly if the local government is paying more of the cost or is willing to pay additional costs to meet other goals. Local governments may be particularly interested in 'recreation-induced regional economic development', but this is traditionally viewed as a transfer by the Corps and not an increase in national income (New England Division of the Corps of Engineers, 1993, p. 36). Cross-agency, cross-jurisdiction projects with multiple funding sources can be challenging but may be part of the future of integrating natural approaches into flood-risk management.

Acknowledgement

I would like to thank, without implicating, Leonard Shabman and Margaret Walls for helpful discussions and comments on earlier drafts of this paper. I would like to thank the National Academies Keck Futures Initiative for funding this work.

Notes

1. In addition, interest has been growing in so-called green infrastructure, a term that largely refers to land use changes designed to increase infiltration of stormwater. This paper focuses on managing large riverine flood events, not managing stormwater, although there could be overlaps in the policies and approaches.
2. Personal communication with the chief of the Planning Branch of the New England Division of the Corps of Engineers indicates that no natural storage projects have been undertaken since the Charles River case. However, the Corps has used other nonstructural approaches to flood-risk reduction.
3. A report for the Charles River case highlighted three related, but slightly different, criteria for NVS preservation to be recommended as the preferred alternative: (1) extensive NVS still in existence, (2) currently only minor flood damage, and (3) an imminent threat to the loss of NVS (New England Division of the Corps of Engineers, 1976a).
4. Or for restoration projects, which would similarly be adding new protection.
5. Also of note, if a much lower discount rate had been used, this also would make the benefits greater than costs in the Spicket case, again highlighting the important role of the choice of a discount rate in long-lived projects.
6. The report presented details on the assumptions for each river reach.

7. For example, in 2013, FEMA issued mitigation policy FP-108-024-01, which allowed for inclusion of environmental benefits in benefit-cost analysis of property acquisition projects (buyouts).
8. An economic analysis of a greenway along a river in St. Louis County, Missouri found that avoided flood damages alone did not exceed the opportunity costs of land acquisition, but when other benefits were included, the total benefits exceeded costs (Kousky & Walls, 2014).
9. For more information on these projects see: http://www.countyofnapa.org/Pages/ DepartmentContent.aspx?id=4294971816; http://www.truckeeflood.us/; and http://www.trini tyrivercorridor.com/flood-control/dallas-floodway-project.html.

References

Barham, E. (2001). Ecological boundaries as community boundaries: The politics of watersheds. *Society & Natural Resources: An International Journal, 14*(3), 181–191. doi:10.1080/ 08941920119376

Buss, L. S. (2005). Nonstructural flood damage reduction within the U.S. army corps of engineers. *Journal of Contemporary Water Research & Education, 130*(1), 26–30. doi:10.1111/j.1936-704X.2005.mp130001005.x

Carter, N. T., & Stern, C. V. (2011). *Army corps of engineers water resources projects: Authorization and appropriations.* Washington, DC: Congressional Research Service.

Chandler, J. P., & Doyle, A. F. (1978). An alliance with nature. *Water Spectrum, 10*(Summer), 24–30.

Cheney, P. B. (1974). *The formulation and evaluation of specific alternatives for flood plain and flood damage management: A report to the new england river basins commission, connecticut river basin program, supplemental flood management study.* Washington, DC: Cheney, Miller, Ellis and Associates.

De Laney, T. A. (1995). Benefits to downstream flood attenuation and water quality as a result of constructed wetlands in agricultural landscapes. *Journal of Soil and Water Conservation, 50*(6), 620–626.

Environmental Protection Agency. (2006). *Wetlands: Protecting life and property from flooding.* Washington, DC: United States Environmental Protection Agency Office of Water.

Galloway, G. E. (2005). Corps of engineers responses to the changing national approach to flood-plain management since the 1993 midwest flood. *Journal of Contemporary Water Research & Education, 130*, 5–12. doi:10.1111/j.1936-704X.2005.mp130001002.x

Heal, G., Daily, G. C., Ehrlich, P. R., Salzman, J., Boggs, C., Hellmann, J., Hughes, J., Kremen, C., & Rickets, T. (2001). Protecting natural capital through ecosystem service districts. *Stanford Environmental Law Journal, 20*, 333–364.

Kousky, C. (2010). Using natural capital to reduce disaster risk. *Journal of Natural Resources Policy Research, 2*(4), 343–356. doi:10.1080/19390459.2010.511451

Kousky, C., & Walls, M. (2014). Floodplain conservation as a flood mitigation strategy: Examining costs and benefits. *Ecological Economics, 104*, 119–128. doi:10.1016/j.ecolecon.2014.05.001

Kousky, C., & Zeckhauser, R. (2006). JARring Actions that Fuel the Floods. In R. J. Daniels, D. F. Kettle, & H. Kunreuther (Eds.), *On risk and disaster: Lessons from hurricane katrina* (pp. 59–73). Philedelphia: University of Pennsylvania Press.

Landy, M. (2008). Mega-disasters and federalism. *Public Administration Review, 68*, S186–S198. doi:10.1111/j.1540-6210.2008.00988.x

Larson, W. M., & Dingman, S. L. (1981). *The potential for flood-damage reduction through preservation of natural valley storage in the piscataqua river basin.* Durham: University of New Hampshire.

Merz, B., Kreibich, H., Thieken, A., & Schmidtke, R. (2004). Estimation uncertainty of direct monetary flood damage to buildings. *Natural Hazards and Earth System Sciences, 4*, 153–163. doi:10.5194/nhess-4-153-2004

Murray, B. C., Sohngen, B., & Ross, M. T. (2007). Economic consequences of consideration of permanence, leakage, and additionality for soil carbon sequestration projects. *Climatic Change, 80*(1–2), 127–143. doi:10.1007/s10584-006-9169-4

National Research Council. (1999). New Directions in Water Resources Planning for the U.S. Army Corps of Engineers. Washington, DC: Committee to Assess the U.S. Army Corps of Engineers Water Resources Project Planning Procedures.

New England Division of the Corps of Engineers. (1972). *Charles river, massachusetts: Main report and attachments*. Waltham, MA: Department of the Army, New England Division, Corps of Engineers.

New England Division of the Corps of Engineers. (1976a). *Water resources development plan: Charles river watershed, massachusetts*. Waltham, MA: Department of the Army, New England Division, Corps of Engineers.

New England Division of the Corps of Engineers. (1976b). *Water resources development plan: Charles river watershed, natural valley storage project, design memorandum no. 2, phase I–phase II combined, general description*. Waltham, MA: Department of the Army, New England Division, Corps of Engineers.

New England Division of the Corps of Engineers. (1976c). *Water resources development plan: Charles river watershed, natural valley storage areas project, massachusetts, design memorandum no. 3, real estate*. Waltham, MA: Department of the Army, New England Division, Corps of Engineers.

New England Division of the Corps of Engineers. (1978a). *Assessment of the flood problems of the taunton river basin in massachusetts*. Waltham, MA: Department of the Army, New England Division, Corps of Engineers.

New England Division of the Corps of Engineers. (1978b). *Natural valley storage: A partnership with nature*. Public Information Fact Sheet. Waltham, MA: Department of the Army, New England Division, Corps of Engineers.

New England Division of the Corps of Engineers. (1979). *Neponset river basin flood plain management study: Reconnaissance report*. Waltham, MA: Department of the Army, New England Division, Corps of Engineers.

New England Division of the Corps of Engineers. (1982). *Neponset river basin, massachusetts, flood plain management study: Water resources investigation review draft*. Waltham, MA: Department of the Army, New England Division, Corps of Engineers.

New England Division of the Corps of Engineers. (1990). *Spicket river basin study: General investigation study, spicket river basin, massachusetts and new hampshire*. Waltham, MA: Department of the Army, New England Division, Corps of Engineers.

New England Division of the Corps of Engineers. (1993). *Massachusetts natural valley storage investigation: Section 22 study*. Waltham, MA: US Army Corps of Engineers and Commonwealth of Massachusetts, Executive Office of Environmental Affairs.

New England Division of the Corps of Engineers. (1994). *Water resources study reconnaissance report: Connecticut river basin natural valley storage: connecticut, massachusetts, new hampshire and vermont*. Waltham, MA: Department of the Army, New England Division, Corps of Engineers.

Opperman, J. J., Galloway, G. E., Fargione, J., Mount, J. F., Richter, B. D., & Secchi, S. (2009). Sustainable floodplains through large-scale reconnection to rivers. *Science, 326*(5959), 1487–1488. doi:10.1126/science.1178256

Platt, R. H., & McMullen, G. M. (1979). *Fragmentation of public authority over floodplains: The charles river case*. Amherst: Water Resources Research Center, University of Massachusetts.

Platt, R. H., Salvesen, D., & Baldwin, G. H. B. (2002). Rebuilding the North Carolina coast after hurricane fran: Did public regulations matter? *Coastal Management, 30*, 249–269. doi:10.1080/08920750290042192

Potter, K. W. (1994). Estimating potential reduction flood benefits of restored wetlands. *Water Resources Update, 97*(Autumn), 34–38.

Powers, K. (2003). *Benefit–cost analysis and the discount rate for the corps of engineers' water resource projects: Theory and practice*. Washington, DC: Congressional Research Service.

Shabman, L. A. 1972. *Decision Making in Water Resource Investment and the Potential of Multi-Objective Planning: The Case of the Army Corps of Engineers* (Technical Report 42). Ithaca, NY: Cornell University Water Resources and Marine Sciences Center.

Shabman, L., & Scodari, P. 2012. Towards Integrated Water Reesources Management: A Conceptual Framework for U.S. Army Corps of Engineers Water and Related Land Resources Implementation Studies, Institute for Water Resources.

Valderrama, A., Levine, L., bloomgarden, E., Bayon, R., Wachowicz, K., & Kaiser, C. (2013). *Creating clean water cash flows: Developing private markets for green stormwater infrastructure in philadelphia*. Washington, DC: Natural Resources Defense Council.

Wunder, S. (2007). The efficiency of payments for environmental services in tropical conservation. *Conservation Biology, 21*(1), 48–58. doi:10.1111/j.1523-1739.2006.00559.x

Probabilistic forecasting and the reshaping of flood risk management

Sarah Michaels

Department of Political Science, Faculty Fellow, Public Policy Center, University of Nebraska, Lincoln, NE USA

Advances in probabilistic forecasting, notably based on ensemble prediction systems, are transforming flood risk management. Four trends shaping the assimilation of probabilistic flood forecasting into flood risk management are longer forecasting lead times, advances in decision-making aids, inclusion of probabilistic forecasting in hazard mitigation and collaboration between researchers and managers. Confronting how to use probabilistic flood forecasts to make binary management decisions for reducing flood losses requires developing institutional capacity while acknowledging flood risk estimation is one component of decision making under uncertainty in an evolving policy landscape.

1. Introduction

Advances in probabilistic forecasting are altering flood risk management profoundly. Forecasting, for de Franco and Meyer (2011), consists of all activities people engage in to make sense of the future. Since any 'rational' policy of prevention or mitigation is based on knowledge claims about what will happen and what the consequences will be, they consider forecasting to be an essential management activity. Yet, with notable exceptions, such as Dale et al. (2014), Demeritt, Nobert, Cloke, and Pappenberger (2013), Demeritt, Nobert, Cloke, and Pappenberger (2010), and Stephens and Cloke (2014), much of the discussion on forecasting focuses on scientific and technical advances rather than on the prospect for appropriately and effectively incorporating them into flood risk management. What counts when it comes to information is not the information *per se,* rather it is how the information is used (Ramos, Mathevet, Thielen, & Pappenberger, 2010). Consequently, the contribution of this paper is to set out from a practitioner perspective some key considerations in the current state of employing probabilistic flood forecasting in flood risk management.

To get the most out of flood forecasting requires understanding and quantifying the associated uncertainties curtailing their operational value (Schumann, Wang, & Dietrich, 2011). Yet making and living with the consequences of specific, binary decisions on behalf of others, such as whether to close floodgates or to issue a flood warning, based on probabilistic information, is not easy. This is especially so when the outcome of a decision appears as a mismatch with the reality experienced; for example, failing to issue a flood warning when serious flooding occurs.

Using probabilistic forecasting to operationalize risk as a core decision-making criterion involves considering the odds an outcome will happen and the consequences of that outcome. In probabilistic flood forecasting, two components are involved: (1) estimating the spectrum of potential peak levels of water predicted, which determines the likelihood of flooding, and (2) determining the impact of flooding caused when water reaches the predicted levels (Dale et al., 2014).

Ensemble forecasts, by distinguishing where forecast uncertainties come from (Schumann et al., 2011), are one means for formally incorporating uncertainty (Pagano, Shrestha, Wang, Robertson, & Hapuarachchi, 2013). Ensemble forecast systems indicate uncertainties in input data, parameters, and models (Schumann et al., 2011); they are run many times, each time beginning with slightly altered starting conditions and with small perturbations to the model (Bowler, Arribas, Mylne, Robertson, & Beare, 2008; Cloke & Pappenberger, 2009). Rather than generating one value for the variable being investigated, a range of values are created (Dietrich, Denhard, & Schumann, 2009). Data and information generated by imperfect models and uncertain data can be merged using ensembles (Schumann et al., 2011). A key intent of ensemble flood forecasting is to array the complete range of forecast uncertainty and/or predictability by presenting various hydrological responses to different inputs generated from atmospheric ensemble prediction systems (Zappa, Fundel, & Jaun, 2013). Since not all forecast users have the same risk tolerance, ensemble prediction systems are useful because they generate information applicable to different decision thresholds. For the same flood event, different people experience different costs of flooding (Pappenberger, Cloke, et al. 2011). For example, a user confronted by high costs of taking protective action compared to prospective loss may well require more certainty to act than a user facing a lower ratio (Zhu, Toth, Wobus, Richardson, & Mylne, 2002).

Advances in probabilistic flood forecasting are among the converging circumstances making it timely to consider the implications for flood risk management of incorporating flood forecasting uncertainties. These are discussed in the next section followed by an examination of what makes forecasts with uncertainty useful to practitioners. After that, four trends shaping the incorporation of probabilistic forecasting into flood risk management are identified. Before concluding, selected challenges facing practitioners interested in incorporating probabilistic forecasting into flood risk management are reviewed.

2. Why it is timely to consider incorporating flood forecasting uncertainties in flood risk management

A convergence of five circumstances makes it timely to consider the implications for flood management of incorporating uncertainties in flood forecasting.

(1) People and property are increasingly exposed to flooding (Gopalakrishnan, 2013; Stephens & Cloke, 2014; United Nations International Strategy for Disaster Reduction [UNISDR], 2012). There is mounting concern about how vulnerable water resources are to fast-changing conditions and our collective capacity to mitigate the impacts of extreme events on what people care about (Ramos, van Andel, & Pappenberger, 2013).

(2) Capabilities for forecasting are improving (UNISDR, 2012). More attention is being paid to how ensemble prediction systems can be used to advance operational flood warning and flood risk management (Cloke & Pappenberger, 2009; Demeritt et al., 2013). Lessons are being drawn from the successful use of

ensemble prediction systems in weather forecasting (Cloke & Pappenberger, 2009) and climate prediction (Collins, 2007). Consequently, beginning in the late 1990s, hydrological applications of ensemble-based meteorological forecasts have been developed (Schumann et al., 2011). Doing so captures such benefits as improving forecasting skill (Nobert, Demeritt, & Cloke, 2010). For hydrological ensemble prediction systems (HEPS) this means extending the lead-time for predicting floods (Pappenberger et al., 2013). Especially over the medium range of 3–10 days, ensemble prediction systems demonstrate greater skill than conventional deterministic forecasting systems in forecasting rainfall and related fluvial flooding (Richardson, 2000; Roulin, 2007; Pappenberger, Thielen, & Del Medico, 2011).

To advance operational water management and better anticipate hydrologic extremes, meteorological and hydrologic prediction models have been coupled. Based on these coupled models, forecasting and warning systems have been developed to improve flood and drought risk planning and response, and to optimize managing and regulating water use for purposes ranging from domestic consumption to supplying thermal power plants (Ramos et al., 2013).

Advances in applying ensemble prediction systems to flood forecasting may give people more confidence in forecasts and make them more willing to act on forecasts than they are currently (Demeritt et al., 2010). Still, applying meteorological ensemble forecasts to flood forecasting is not unproblematic. For example, there are few options to validate them because data is limited and the reforecasting of past flood events is costly (Schumann et al., 2011). Generating large ensembles is restricted by the extent of model complexity and high model resolution (Curry & Webster, 2011). Probabilistic techniques are often focused on selected sources of uncertainty, such as in model parameters, and on reducing them in selective ways (Pappenberger & Brown, 2013). As a result, the uncertainties of models are not fully represented by ensemble forecasting systems (Schumann et al., 2011). Advances in post-processing of forecasts are making headway, however, in ameliorating this situation (Cloke et al., 2013). Nonetheless, methods and techniques to cascade uncertainties are not yet fully developed and tested in operational meteohydrology (Ramos et al., 2010).

(3) The scientific community envisions contributing to improved decision making by providing users with probabilistic weather information (Marimo, Kaplan, Mylne, & Sharpe, 2012). Indeed forecasts that do not include uncertainty information are now considered incomplete. Providing an estimate of uncertainty is regarded as being as important as increasing accuracy and timeliness (National Research Council, 2006). The weather, climate and hydrology communities are more interested in effectively conveying uncertainty as the capacity to estimate uncertainty in hydro-meteorological forecasts has improved (National Research Council, 2006; Pappenberger & Beven, 2006). Part of this enlarged capacity stems from employing an increasingly broad array of models in a framework for estimating uncertainty. This has been made possible by greater capacity in computational power, parallel processes, and software (Juston et al., 2013).

(4) At the turn of the twenty-first century there has been notable progress in understanding how individuals grasp uncertainty and probabilistic information (Marx et al., 2007). What is becoming apparent through empirical research is study participants make better decisions when provided with information about uncertainty than when they are not provided with it (Marimo et al., 2012; Roulston & Kaplan, 2009).

(5) Decision makers are expressing interest in gaining a sense of the range of uncertainties they face and the risks associated with the consequences of their choices (Pappenberger & Beven, 2006). Civil protection authorities will employ ensemble prediction systems if they can see how these systems will help optimize their operational options for managing risk (Nobert et al., 2010). Users prefer to make their own situational assessments, and as demonstrated by the public's preference when it comes to weather forecasts, do appreciate probabilistic information (Frick & Hegg, 2011; Handmer & Proudley, 2007). The use of probabilistic flood forecasts is in tune with the wider trend in public policy to employ risk-based decision making. For example, the United Kingdom government has been a leading proponent of embedding risk as a core decision-making consideration (Rothstein & Downer, 2012), thereby making risk management an integral component of government planning (Massey & Rentoul, 2007).

3. Making forecasts with uncertainty useful to practitioners

When users receive a forecast including upper and lower bounds of the predictive interval they may conclude forecast providers acknowledge the forecast's uncertainty and still consider taking protective action is justified. This is particularly important for extreme events when it is vital for people to trust the forecast and to take the recommended actions (Joslyn, Savelli, & Nadav-Greenberg, 2011). A key determinant of the palatability of warnings to decision makers is whether or not they perceive there are feasible actions they can take at a cost they can afford (Meyer & de Franco, 2011).

When people are not provided with estimates of forecast uncertainty they attempt to take uncertainty into account on their own (Joslyn et al., 2011). In doing so they may make serious errors (Joslyn & Savelli, 2010). Ramos et al. (2013) found when people are not provided with uncertainty information, they move towards risk-averse positions.

Providing uncertainty information contributes to more optimal decisions and tends to result in individuals making convergent decisions (Ramos et al., 2013). Conveying the uncertainties surrounding scientific knowledge and admitting the limitations of that knowledge helps gain and retain decision makers' and the public's trust (Juston et al., 2013; Ramos et al., 2013).

While technical qualities provide one framework for assessing the overall value of hydrometeorological forecasts, a second framework emphasizing functional qualities, such as how forecast products, characteristics and metrics are communicated (Buizza et al., 2007) is of direct interest to decision makers. Forecast system utility is about measuring how valuable forecasts are for practical applications. This depends on forecast system attributes such as space-time scale and quality. Are forecasts issued at usable scales and lead-time? Are they provided in a timely manner? Are uncertainties communicated appropriately? (Pappenberger & Brown, 2013). What will help increase the use of probabilistic forecasts generated by ensemble prediction systems are advances in how these forecasts are presented and the means to evaluate the ensemble forecasts from the users' perspectives (Cloke et al., 2013). The value of a forecast is a function of the extent to which it shapes decisions where uncertainty is a major concern (Handmer & Proudley, 2007; Murphy, 1993). Ultimately what matters is the extent to which a forecast results in benefits accrued, or losses avoided, that would not have occurred if it was not employed (Schumann et al., 2011; Zhu et al., 2002).

Different users make use of different forecasts. Given the array of needs, users value forecasts they can adapt appropriately to their individual circumstances (Handmer &

Proudley, 2007 citing McDavitt, 1998). Ideally, ensemble-based operational flood management systems should reflect the differing needs different operational functions, such as controlling reservoirs, releasing flood warnings, and triggering flood defense measures, have for varying extents of forecast accuracy and lead times (Dietrich et al., 2009). Total discharge volume forecasts are valuable to lake managers and hydropower dam operators. For flood planning and relief, the timing of peak flow and volume of peak discharge are key (Zappa et al., 2013). Reservoir management and early warning systems for potential extreme flood events make use of medium-range forecasts with lead times of 3–5 days. Flood alerts are delivered, and flood defense measures are initiated, based on short to very short-range forecasts that include detailed information about peak time, peak discharge and possible inundation areas, and into which observed data can be assimilated. Hydrological uncertainty is a critical consideration in short-range forecasting (Schumann et al., 2011).

Under a number of circumstances decisions based on probabilistic rather than deterministic forecasts are advantageous. Yet it is less clear whether this holds when forecast error increases or action is required when the probability of an event occurring is low. While there are benefits to quantifying uncertainty in many circumstances, emergency managers contend that, when the probability of an adverse weather event is low, specifying the low probability will discourage compliance with warnings. For example, to enable a successful evacuation severe weather warnings must be released early. Yet, the probability of adverse weather in a given region may be less than 20% just a few days before the event is anticipated to strike. It is tempting for decision makers to withhold uncertainty information because of the perceived need to reduce the complexity of information being presented (Joslyn et al., 2011). It is unclear, though, whether better decisions are procured by providing people with uncertainty forecasts or by providing them with explicit instructions (Joslyn & LeClerc, 2012).

4. Trends to watch

The world of incorporating probabilistic forecasting into flood risk management is fast evolving. Four trends are contributing to the shape and pace of this evolution.

(1) Creating longer forecast lead times provides an essential underpinning for improving early warning systems, investing in flood mitigation, advancing preparedness and furthering risk awareness. One promising means for doing so in hydrological forecasting is using coupled meteohydrological forecasting systems (Ramos et al., 2010).

(2) While decision-making aids for exploiting probabilistic flood forecasting are in their infancy (Dale et al., 2014), the search is on for promising means to incorporate new decision support technologies into practice (Demeritt et al., 2010; Frick & Hegg, 2011). This includes how to assimilate ensemble prediction systems, touted as the best available science for operational flood forecasting, effectively and appropriately into decision support for flood risk management (Demeritt et al., 2013). If forecasts are to be valuable in time-sensitive situations, such as managing flood incidents, developing visualization tools and forecast products that effectively and appropriately convey uncertainty becomes critical (Cloke et al., 2013).

(3) While much attention has focused understandably on using probabilistic flood forecasting for real time flood management (Cloke et al., 2013), incorporating

such forecasting into long-term hazard mitigation and adaptation will have profound implications. For example, the full potential of incorporating ensemble models into maps indicating risk to floodplains has yet to be realized. In the immediate, the inherent uncertainty in these maps pose challenges for planners (Faulkner, Parker, Green, & Beven, 2007) and others attempting to use them to guide decision making.

(4) Reflecting a broad trend towards inclusive decision making, there is growing interest in collaboration as an important means for incorporating probabilistic forecasting into flood risk management. Collaboration ideally involves scientists, forecasters and end-users (Pappenberger, Cloke, et al. 2011). A powerful reason to collaborate is to provide operational forecasts predicting the variables of greatest salience to the decision being made in the form and time scale of most value to users (Wilks, 1997). It is also helpful if joint decisions are made by producers and users about how to illustrate and demonstrate inconsistency in forecast products (Pappenberger, Cloke, et al. 2011).

The process of designing ensemble prediction systems benefits from users being involved in the very early stages (Nobert et al., 2010). Likewise it is valuable for information providers to partner with the decision maker to reach decisions using the new information. A prerequisite is having information providers appreciate how the targeted recipients interpret and intend to use the information received (Morss, Lazo, & Demuth, 2010) and how the information contributes to shaping the decision makers' beliefs.

How probabilistic forecasts can be communicated effectively to nonscientists engaged in flood risk reduction is still being worked out (Nobert et al., 2010). While promising visualization tools are being employed, there are not yet agreed upon best-practices for communicating ensemble flood forecasts. This reflects both (1) the relative novelty of such flood forecasts (Lumbroso & von Christierson, 2009) and (2) the lag between generating the science and its utilization. An overarching frustration is the delay between gains in forecasting and the uptake of state of the science forecasts by decision makers (Demeritt et al., 2013).

5. Challenges

Technical challenges remain in designing and generating ensemble prediction systems for flood forecasts (Cloke & Pappenberger, 2009; Demeritt et al., 2010; Ramos et al., 2010). Our interest in this paper, however, is on challenges to incorporating probabilistic forecasts into flood risk management from the vantage of practitioners. However uncertain is the forecasting, flood managers must make categorical decisions for specific places often in a pressurized setting, frequently in advance of a potentially damaging event (Cloke & Pappenberger, 2009; Dale et al., 2014). For example, managers must decide whether to close flood gates or not, to erect temporary flood barriers or not, to issue warnings or not (Dale et al., 2014; Penning-Rowsell, Tunstall, Tapsell, & Parker, 2000; Werner, Cranston, Harrison, Whitfield, & Schellekens, 2009). The question for decision makers in such circumstances is how in real-time to use probabilistic flood forecasts to make binary decisions. Practitioners must choose which one or a combination of forecasts from among the range of possible probabilistic forecasts is most helpful in addressing a particular decision (Dale et al., 2014). Probability-based decision making is challenging in the context of situation-specific settings (Handmer & Proudley, 2007). It is one reason

Nobert et al. (2010) recommend ensemble prediction system training be custom designed and delivered locally.

Moving to probabilistic forecasting from deterministic forecasting may trigger an institutional shift in who is responsible for decision making under uncertainty (Dale et al., 2014). Who owns the uncertainty judgment has implications for the relationship between forecast producers and users. The outcome determines who will be blamed (De Franco & Meyer, 2011).

Accountability is also a concern among forecast producers. National flood forecasting agencies in Europe that have public safety statutory mandates and value certainty over advance notice may be cautious about employing the European Commission's European Flood Alert System (EFAS) alerts generated from medium-term ensemble forecasts. They are concerned about being held responsible if EFAS alerts are wrong (Demeritt & Nobert, 2011).

Interpreting flood forecast uncertainties generated through the scientific enterprise may not be a responsibility with which those who have not generated the forecasts are comfortable. Practitioners may be reluctant to interpret uncertainty tools (Faulkner et al., 2007 citing Handmer et al., 2003). Emergency managers may struggle at the outset to understand probabilistic forecasts especially when probabilistic forecasts may seem to be at odds with what some flood professionals regard as their primary need, accurate information (McCarthy, Tunstall, Parker, Faulkner, & Howe, 2007).

While operational flood forecasters seek greater certainty at the local scale, medium-term forecasts by their construction are coarse in scale and often uncertain. Forecasters confront the tension between competing and incompatible policy demands for earlier warnings and more certain ones. The uncertainty of medium-term flood forecasts requires users to weigh the opportunity costs of precautionary action and false alarms. While advances in ensemble prediction systems hold out the promise of increasing the predictability and foresight offered by medium-range (3–7 days) forecasts, what is not in place is the institutional capacity to utilize fully such forecast outputs in flood risk management (Demeritt et al., 2013).

As flood forecasters understand it, the preferences of those in civil protection authorities is for 'deterministic forecasts issued with a high degree of certainty' (Demeritt et al., 2013, p. 155). This reflects an institutional culture seeking to avoid false alarms, and the associated harmed reputations and disinclination of individuals to respond to future warnings (Nobert et al., 2010). There is concern a series of false alarms will result in individuals no longer responding to warnings and in so doing increase the consequences of a damaging event when it does happen. Conversely, a failure to warn individuals about a flood event that does occur can be devastating to those directly impacted by the flooding and for the authority that did not provide the alert (Dedieu, 2010).

Institutional mandates understandably dictate what staff members emphasize. For example, historically European flood forecasting agencies because of their public safety statutory responsibility focused on very short term warnings in the zero to 48 hour range to facilitate public evacuation rather than medium-term forecasting valuable for mitigating flood damage. This responsibility meant that, when it came to issuing flood warnings, they set high confidence thresholds more achievable in the very short term than for longer time horizons (Demeritt et al., 2013).

Estimating flood risk is one component of the wider challenge of making decisions under uncertainty in an evolving policy landscape (Faulkner et al., 2007). For example, to incorporate climate change into planning activities, water managers must include uncertain information derived from a range of projections from climate models into the management and operation models they already use. Uncertainty around individual considerations increases concurrently with consideration over time of different issues (Barsugli et al., 2012). Flood risk managers must consider the natural indeterminism of whether a flood will occur or not, along with associated social indeterminism, such as how an issued warning will be interpreted and the implications of an issued warning not being justified (Demeritt et al., 2010; Michaels & Tyre, 2012). Uncertainty about human behavior may result from the diverse perspectives individuals and communities bring to the situations they face. It may also be a function of conflicting interests, varying standards for evidence, and differing degrees of risk aversion (Casman, Morgan, & Dowlatabadi, 1999; Morgan, 1998; Moss, 2007).

People with different attitudes process evidence, including uncertain and conflicting evidence, in different ways (Corner, Whitmarsh, & Xenias, 2012). The critical point for forecasts is the one at which individuals alter their plans (Handmer & Proudley, 2007); however, there may not be a universal critical point. In making tradeoffs required in decision making, such as between current and future risks, people may benefit less from more facts and more from different perspectives that help them clarify the implications of a decision on what they value (Pidgeon & Fischhoff, 2011).

6. Conclusion

Our ability to leverage the considerable advances in probabilistic flood forecasting is contingent on being able to apply them in decisions that ultimately reduce losses from flood risk. From a practitioner perspective, one of the most demanding aspects of applying probabilistic forecasting is how to consider constructively the uncertainty articulated in such forecasts. Doing so involves reconfiguring entrenched patterns of interaction between model developers, model users, those making decisions based on model outputs, and those affected by such decisions. With earlier, deterministic models it was easier to consider that a linear approach to forecast transmission was adequate and to down play subjective considerations, such as risk tolerance. With probabilistic forecasts generating a range of possibilities, the advantages of ongoing interaction between development, use and exploitation of forecasts come to the fore. Probabilistic forecasting highlights there is no single output satisfying the needs of all users. A critical, ongoing search in practitioner-engaged probabilistic forecasting is underway to develop forecasts that generate the outputs needed for decision making. In the long lead-up to this ideal state, we must explore how best to bridge what we can do with what is needed.

Acknowledgements

The research for this paper was made possible with faculty development leave support from the University of Nebraska-Lincoln and a faculty fellowship from the Advanced Study Program, National Center for Atmospheric Research, Boulder, Colorado. Three anonymous reviewers provided constructive comments on an earlier draft and Dr. Dannele Peck, Associate Editor, *Journal of Natural Resources Policy Research* provided technical editing.

References

Barsugli, J. J., Vogel, J. M., Kaatz, L., Smith, J. B., Waage, M., & Anderson, C. J. (2012). Two faces of uncertainty: Climate science and water utility planning methods. *Journal of Water Resources Planning and Management, 138*(5), 389–395. doi:10.1061/(ASCE)WR.1943-5452.0000188

Bowler, N. E., Arribas, A., Mylne, K. R., Robertson, K. B., & Beare, S. E. (2008). The MOGREPS short-range ensemble prediction system. *Quarterly Journal of the Royal Meteorological Society, 134*(632), 703–722. doi:10.1002/qj.234

Buizza, R., Asensio, H., Balint, G., Bartholmes, J., Bliefernicht, J., Bogner, K., ... Vincendon, B. (2007). *EURORISK/PREVIEW report on the technical quality, functional quality and forecast value of meteorological and hydrological forecasts.* Shinfield Park, Reading, UK: European Centre for Medium-Range Weather Forecasts. Retrieved from http://old.ecmwf.int/publications/library/ecpublications/_pdf/tm/501-600/tm516.pdf

Casman, E. A., Morgan, M. G., & Dowlatabadi, H. (1999). Mixed levels of uncertainty in complex policy models. *Risk Analysis, 19*(1), 33–42. doi:10.1111/j.1539-6924.1999.tb00384.x

Cloke, H. L., & Pappenberger, F. (2009). Ensemble flood forecasting: A review. *Journal of Hydrology, 375*(3–4), 613–626. doi:10.1016/j.jhydrol.2009.06.005

Cloke, H. L., Pappenberger, F., van Andel, S. J., Schaake, J., Thielen, J., & Ramos, M.-H. (Eds.). (2013). Hydrological ensemble prediction systems: Preface. *Hydrological Processes, 27*(1), 1–4. doi:10.1002/hyp.9679

Collins, M. (2007). Ensembles and probabilities: A new era in the prediction of climate change. *Philosophical Transactions of the Royal Society A: Mathematical, Physical and Engineering Sciences, 365*(1857), 1957–1970. doi:10.1098/rsta.2007.2068

Corner, A., Whitmarsh, L., & Xenias, D. (2012). Uncertainty, scepticism and attitudes towards climate change: Biased assimilation and attitude polarisation. *Climatic Change, 114*(3–4), 463–478. doi:10.1007/s10584-012-0424-6

Curry, J. A., & Webster, P. J. (2011). Climate science and the uncertainty monster. *Bulletin of the American Meteorological Society, 92*(12), 1667–1682. doi:10.1175/2011BAMS3139.1

Dale, M., Wicks, J., Mylne, K., Pappenberger, F., Laeger, S., & Taylor, S. (2014). Probabilistic flood forecasting and decision-making: An innovative risk-based approach. *Natural Hazards, 70*(1), 159–172. doi:10.1007/s11069-012-0483-z

De Franco, C., & Meyer, C. O. (2011). Introduction: The challenges of prevention. In C. O. Meyer (Ed.), *Forecasting, warning and responding to transnational risks* (pp. 1–19). Basingstoke, Hampshire, UK: Palgrave MacMillan.

Dedieu, F. (2010). Alerts and catastrophes: The case of the 1999 storm in France, a treacherous risk. *Sociologie Du Travail, 52*(Supplement 1), e1–e21. doi:10.1016/j.soctra.2010.06.001

Demeritt, D., & Nobert, S. (2011). Responding to early flood warnings in the European Union. In C. O. Meyer & C. de Franco (Eds.), *Forecasting, warning and responding to transnational risks* (pp. 127–147). Basingstoke, Hampshire, UK: Palgrave MacMillan.

Demeritt, D., Nobert, S., Cloke, H., & Pappenberger, F. (2010). Challenges in communicating and using ensembles in operational flood forecasting. *Meteorological Applications, 17*(2), 209–222. doi:10.1002/met.194

Demeritt, D., Nobert, S., Cloke, H. L., & Pappenberger, F. (2013). The European flood alert system and the communication, perception, and use of ensemble predictions for operational flood risk management. *Hydrological Processes, 27*(1), 147–157. doi:10.1002/hyp.9419

Dietrich, J., Denhard, M., & Schumann, A. H. (2009). Can ensemble forecasts improve the reliability of flood alerts? *Journal of Flood Risk Management, 2*(4), 232–242. doi:10.1111/j.1753-318X.2009.01039.x

Faulkner, H., Parker, D., Green, C., & Beven, K. (2007). Developing a translational discourse to communicate uncertainty in flood risk between science and the practitioner. *AMBIO: A Journal of the Human Environment, 36*(8), 692–704. doi:10.1579/0044-7447(2007)36[692:DATDTC]2.0.CO;2

Frick, J., & Hegg, C. (2011). Can end-users' flood management decision making be improved by information about forecast uncertainty? *Atmospheric Research, 100*(2–3), 296–303. doi:10.1016/j.atmosres.2010.12.006

Gopalakrishnan, C. (2013). Water and disasters: A review and analysis of policy aspects. *International Journal of Water Resources Development, 29*(2), 250–271. doi:10.1080/07900627.2012.756133

Handmer, J., & Proudley, B. (2007). Communicating uncertainty via probabilities: The case of weather forecasts. *Environmental Hazards, 7*(2), 79–87. doi:10.1016/j.envhaz.2007.05.002

Joslyn, S., & Savelli, S. (2010). Communicating forecast uncertainty: Public perception of weather forecast uncertainty. *Meteorological Applications, 17*(2), 180–195. doi:10.1002/met.190

Joslyn, S. L., & LeClerc, J. E. (2012). Uncertainty forecasts improve weather-related decisions and attenuate the effects of forecast error. *Journal of Experimental Psychology: applied, 18*(1), 126–140. doi:10.1037/a0025185

Joslyn, S., Savelli, S., & Nadav-Greenberg, L. (2011). Reducing probabilistic weather forecasts to the worst-case scenario: Anchoring effects. *Journal of Experimental Psychology: Applied, 17* (4), 342–353. doi:10.1037/a0025901

Juston, J. M., Kauffeldt, A., Montano, B. Q., Seibert, J., Beven, K. J., & Westerberg, I. K. (2013). Smiling in the rain: Seven reasons to be positive about uncertainty in hydrological modelling. *Hydrological Processes, 27*(7), 1117–1122. doi:10.1002/hyp.9625

Lumbroso, D., & von Christierson, B. (2009). *Communication and dissemination of probabilistic flood warnings: Literature review of international material.* Bristol, UK: Environment Agency.

Marimo, P., Kaplan, T. R., Mylne, K., & Sharpe, M. (2012). Communication of uncertainty in weather forecasts. Retrieved from http://mpra.ub.uni-muenchen.de/38287/

Marx, S. M., Weber, E. U., Orlove, B. S., Leiserowitz, A., Krantz, D. H., Roncoli, C., & Phillips, J. (2007). Communication and mental processes: Experiential and analytic processing of uncertain climate information. *Global Environmental Change, 17*(1), 47–58. doi:10.1016/j.gloenvcha. 2006.10.004

Massey, A., & Rentoul, J. (2007). Innovative, flexible and creative policy making. In H. Bochel & S. Duncan (Eds.), *Making policy in theory and practice* (pp. 65–85). Bristol, UK: The Policy Press.

McCarthy, S., Tunstall, S., Parker, D., Faulkner, H., & Howe, J. (2007). Risk communication in emergency response to a simulated extreme flood. *Environmental Hazards, 7*(3), 179–192. doi:10.1016/j.envhaz.2007.06.003

Meyer, C. O., & de Franco, C. (2011). Conclusion: New perspectives for theorising and addressing transnational risks. In C. O. Meyer & C. de Franco (Eds.), *Forecasting, warning and responding to transnational risks* (pp. 241–257). Basingstoke, Hampshire, UK: Palgrave MacMillan.

Michaels, S., & Tyre, A. J. (2012). How indeterminism shapes ecologists' contributions to managing socio-ecological systems. *Conservation Letters, 5*(4), 289–295. doi:10.1111/j.1755-263X.2012. 00241.x

Morgan, M. G. (1998). Uncertainty analysis in risk assessment. *Human and Ecological Risk Assessment, 4*(1), 25–39.

Morss, R. E., Lazo, J. K., & Demuth, J. L. (2010). Examining the use of weather forecasts in decision scenarios: Results from a US survey with implications for uncertainty communication. *Meteorological Applications, 17*(2), 149–162. doi:10.1002/met.196

Moss, R. H. (2007). Improving information for managing an uncertain future climate. *Global Environmental Change, 17*(1), 4–7. doi:10.1016/j.gloenvcha.2006.12.002

Murphy, A. H. (1993). What is a good forecast? An essay on the nature of goodness in weather forecasting. *Weather and Forecasting, 8,* 281–293. doi:10.1175/1520-0434(1993)008<0281: WIAGFA>2.0.CO;2

National Research Council. (2006). *Completing the forecast: Characterizing and communicating uncertainty for better decisions using weather and climate forecasts.* Washington, DC: The National Academies Press.

Nobert, S., Demeritt, D., & Cloke, H. (2010). Informing operational flood management with ensemble predictions: Lessons from Sweden. *Journal of Flood Risk Management, 3*(1), 72–79. doi:10.1111/j.1753-318X.2009.01056.x

Pagano, T. C., Shrestha, D. L., Wang, Q. J., Robertson, D., & Hapuarachchi, P. (2013). Ensemble dressing for hydrological applications. *Hydrological Processes, 27*(1), 106–116. doi:10.1002/ hyp.9313

Pappenberger, F., & Beven, K. J. (2006). Ignorance is bliss: Or seven reasons not to use uncertainty analysis. *Water Resources Research, 42*(5), W05302. doi:10.1029/2005WR004820

Pappenberger, F., & Brown, J. D. (2013). HP today: On the pursuit of (im)perfection in flood forecasting. *Hydrological Processes, 27*(1), 162–163. doi:10.1002/hyp.9465

Pappenberger, F., Cloke, H. L., Persson, A., & Demeritt, D. (2011). On forecast (in)consistency in a hydro-meteorological chain: Curse or blessing? *Hydrology and Earth System Sciences, 15*(7), 2391–2400. doi:10.5194/hess-15-2391-2011

Pappenberger, F., Stephens, E., Thielen, J., Salamon, P., Demeritt, D., van Andel, S. J., & Alfieri, L. (2013). Visualizing probabilistic flood forecast information: Expert preferences and perceptions of best practice in uncertainty communication. *Hydrological Processes, 27*(1), 132–146. doi:10.1002/hyp.9253

Pappenberger, F., Thielen, J., & Del Medico, M. (2011). The impact of weather forecast improvements on large scale hydrology: Analysing a decade of forecasts of the european flood alert system. *Hydrological Processes, 25*(7), 1091–1113. doi:10.1002/hyp.7772

Penning-Rowsell, E. C., Tunstall, S. M., Tapsell, S. M., & Parker, D. J. (2000). The benefits of flood warnings: Real but elusive, and politically significant. *Water and Environment Journal, 14*(1), 7–14. doi:10.1111/j.1747-6593.2000.tb00219.x

Pidgeon, N., & Fischhoff, B. (2011). The role of social and decision sciences in communicating uncertain climate risks. *Nature Climate Change, 1*(1), 35–41. doi:10.1038/nclimate1080

Ramos, M.-H., Mathevet, T., Thielen, J., & Pappenberger, F. (2010). Communicating uncertainty in hydro-meteorological forecasts: Mission impossible? *Meteorological Applications, 17*(2), 223–235. doi:10.1002/met.202

Ramos, M. H., van Andel, S. J., & Pappenberger, F. (2013). Do probabilistic forecasts lead To Better decisions? *Hydrology and Earth System Sciences, 17*(6), 2219–2232. doi:10.5194/hess-17-2219-2013

Richardson, D. S. (2000). Skill and relative economic value of the ECMWF ensemble prediction system. *Quarterly Journal of the Royal Meteorological Society, 126*(563), 649–667. doi:10.1002/qj.49712656313

Rothstein, H., & Downer, J. (2012). Renewing DEFRA': Exploring the emergence of risk-based policymaking in UK central government. *Public Administration, 90*(3), 781–799. doi:10.1111/j.1467-9299.2011.01999.x

Roulin, E. (2007). Skill and relative economic value of medium-range hydrological ensemble predictions. *Hydrology and Earth System Sciences Discussions, 11*(2), 725–737. doi:10.5194/hess-11-725-2007

Roulston, M. S., & Kaplan, T. R. (2009). A laboratory-based study of understanding of uncertainty in 5-day site-specific temperature forecasts. *Meteorological Applications, 16*(2), 237–244. doi:10.1002/met.113

Schumann, A. H., Wang, Y., & Dietrich, J. (2011). Framing uncertainties in flood forecasting with ensembles. In A. H. Schumann (Ed.), *Flood risk assessment and management* (pp. 53–76). Dordrecht, Netherlands: Springer.

Stephens, E., & Cloke, H. (2014). Improving flood forecasts for better flood preparedness in the UK (and beyond). *The Geographical Journal,* doi: 10.1111/geoj.12103

United Nations International Strategy for Disaster Reduction. (2012). A resilient future: UNISDR statement on zero draft of the outcome document of the UN conference on sustainable development (Rio + 20) "The future we want." Geneva, Switzerland: United Nations. Retrieved from http://www.unisdr.org/files/24941_20120124unisdrstatement.pdf

Werner, M., Cranston, M., Harrison, T., Whitfield, D., & Schellekens, J. (2009). Recent developments in operational flood forecasting in England, Wales and Scotland. *Meteorological Applications, 16*(1), 13–22. doi:10.1002/met.124

Wilks, D. S. (1997). Forecast value: Prescriptive decision studies. In R. W. Katz & A. H. Murphy (Eds.), *Economic value of weather and climate forecasts* (pp. 109–145). Cambridge, UK: Cambridge University Press.

Zappa, M., Fundel, F., & Jaun, S. (2013). A 'peak-box' approach for supporting interpretation and verification of operational ensemble peak-flow forecasts: Supporting ensemble peak-flow forecasts. *Hydrological Processes, 27*(1), 117–131. doi:10.1002/hyp.9521

Zhu, Y., Toth, Z., Wobus, R., Richardson, D., & Mylne, K. (2002). The economic value of ensemble-based weather forecasts. *Bulletin of the American Meteorological Society, 83*, 73–83. doi:10.1175/1520-0477(2002)083<0073:TEVOEB>2.3.CO;2

Examining the benefits of collaboration: the Provider-User Matrix for collaborative flood risk management illustrated by the case of the Ljusnan River, Sweden

Beatrice Hedelin[a] and Mattias Hjerpe[b]

[a]Department of Environmental and Life Sciences, Karlstad University, Karlstad, Sweden; [b]Centre for Climate Science and Policy Research, Linköping University, Linköping, Sweden

This paper examines the benefits of collaboration in flood risk management by introducing a Provider-User Matrix. The matrix is illustrated through a Swedish case of polycentric decision-making. In the Swedish case the users have not yet benefited from collaboration-benefits such as a more advanced understanding of the flood response system or from sharing detailed hydrological data; benefits that should be easily implemented. The Provider-User Matrix offers both a more holistic way to study benefits and a way to start raising the efficiency of collaboration, by identifying mismatches between the benefits provided and the benefits that users need.

Introduction

Collaboration is often regarded as a prerequisite for successfully governing issues that require interdisciplinary, inter-sectoral, and integrative approaches. Governance in relation to climate change, water, and flood risks are typical examples of such issues (e.g., Andonova, Betsill, & Bulkeley, 2009; Pahl-Wostl et al., 2007). During the recent decade's governance trend – shifting authority from governments to more polycentric decision-making arrangements such as hybrid, networked, community-based, collaborative, and adaptive governance arrangements – collaborative governance approaches have been developed, tested, and evaluated.

In polycentric governance settings there is a need for collaborative arrangements. We will introduce here a tool for systematic examination of benefits of collaborative activity based on provider and user estimations.[1] While much collaborative research focuses on the providers, that is, the collaborating group itself, the proposed approach supports a broadened empirical basis by including the potential users of the benefits generated by the collaborative activity. Do views of the benefits from collaboration differ between the collaboration providers and the users? Can a broadened perspective help improve the usefulness of the benefits of the collaboration activity, for example, by unearthing new potential benefits? By starting off from the perspective of the benefits of collaboration, this study aims to advance current collaboration efforts by introducing a provider-user matrix. The matrix is illustrated by means of a case study of a polycentric issue – flood risk management – in Sweden.

Collaboration and the issue of benefits

Scholarly interest in collaborative governance approaches has grown steadily in recent decades, and is now well-established in environmental, natural resource management, and public administration research. A vast and growing number of case studies examine how collaboration can be designed and managed by identifying the preconditions for successful collaboration. Keys to successful practice, often derived from reviews of several case studies, are typically: adequate funding and resources, appropriate internal communication and information exchange, team-building factors (e.g., creation of trust among group members, good organization, and good leadership), and developing shared goals and understanding (Ansell & Gash, 2008; Bryan, 2004; Leach & Pelkey, 2001; Margerum, 1999, 2011; Pagdee, Kim, & Daugherty, 2006; Schuett, Selin, & Carr, 2001). These case studies mainly use the collaborating groups as the empirical point of departure, examining them by surveying or interviewing the collaborating group members. The key findings focus on the functionality of the collaborating group itself.

Theories of collaborative approaches to planning and management have also evolved. Generic examples of such theories are Habermas' (1984) rules of communicative rationality, Healey's (1997) ideas of collaborative planning, and Ostrom's (1990) criteria for governing collective goods, while a specific example for water and flood risk management is the framework developed by Hedelin (2007). Based on these theories, the conditions under which collaborative governance prospers can be identified; these conditions include key actor representation in the group, a clearly-defined group mandate, and vertical and horizontal institutional fit. All three conditions are rarely met in the intricate real-world setting of governance arrangements for complex and multi-faceted socio-ecological systems. Here full representation, even theoretically, is difficult to achieve, mandates generally overlap, and institutional relationships are often unclear.

The complexity of the issue to the governed and the difficulty of making collaboration function according to theoretically-derived criteria make the 'how to' emphasis understandable ('How is successful collaboration accomplished?'). The issue of systematic definition of success in terms of the benefits of the collaborative activity is, however, seldom handled in relation to flood risk management specifically and to collaborative planning and management in general. Some studies, however, focus on assessing success. Mainly, these studies define success as tangible outputs such as a flood risk management plan, a levee construction project or the carrying through of a crisis exercise (Leach, Pelkey, & Sabatier, 2002). Some studies also take an interest in less tangible outcomes, such as learning, shared understanding and raised social capital. For example, in a survey of 44 watershed partnerships, Leach and Pelkey (2001) found that success could be measured by factors such as the perceived effects on watershed conditions and on human and social capital, and on the initiation of restoration and monitoring projects.

In most of the studies that concern the issue of benefits, by assessing success, success is defined by the group members themselves, and the focus is on whether the collaborative efforts meet their internally defined goals and objectives (Conley & Moote, 2003; Leach, 2002). Since questions of success and benefits inherently depend on who defines 'success' and 'benefits', a broad basis for assessment would provide a more comprehensive picture. This matter is emphasized by the democratic problem caused by the non-use of democratic criteria when selecting the members of collaborating groups (Agger & Lofgren,

2008; Montin, 2000). Analyzing benefits based solely on the group itself when important stakeholders might not be represented on it obviously has its shortcomings. Therefore, when addressing the benefits of the collaborative activity, the perspectives of actors other than the collaborating group members themselves should also be considered. The fact that a collaborating group works well as a group, or that it has managed to implement a specific measure, does not necessarily imply that the collaboration effort is useful from a broader perspective. For example, for social learning in the collaborating group to be effective from a broader perspective, the knowledge developed must be integrated and used, at least in the organizations participating in the collaborating group. Moreover, if a flood risk mitigation measure is to be effective from a broader perspective, it must be assessed from the river basin and/or cross-sectoral perspectives.

The broader perspective, where benefits are not studied solely from the perspective of the collaborating group itself, is not entirely neglected in the collaboration literature. Ed Weber's (2003) book 'Bringing Society Back In' is an important example, and Thomas M Koontz has also done so in some of his more recent work (e.g., Hardy & Koontz, 2009; Koontz, 2005). These studies show that the functioning of collaboration is highly complex and that the level of benefit varies and is much dependent on context. An interesting example is Campbell, Koontz, and Bonnell (2011) who studied the effects of collaboration on best management practices by comparing two watersheds – one without collaborative activities and one with such activities. They found that on the whole (collaborative participants and non-participants together) there were no differences in the level of best management practices between the two watersheds. When comparing collaborative participants and non-participants within the same watershed however, they found that participants had better management practices than non-participants. This result could have many explanations but it clearly shows that studies focusing on the benefits from collaboration gain from a broader perspective than the group perspective.

If one truly believes that collaboration is important the issue of benefits is crucial and deserves larger attention. A deeper understanding related to benefits, for example, how contextual factors affect them and how they are assessed by actors outside the collaboration, would likely facilitate the proper allocation of funding and resources for collaborative activity – a well-established key criterion for successful collaboration. Moreover, a focus on benefits could also contribute to another well-established key for success – a picture of the goals connected to the collaboration effort – because the actual and potential benefits could be seen as a way to define the goals of the collaboration.

Broadening the perspective: the Provider-User Matrix

One way to develop the understanding of collaboration benefits further is to focus on comparing the 'group' perspective (i.e., the perspective of the participants in the collaborative activity) with the 'user' perspective. A user perspective captures whether the benefits of the collaborative activity are put into action, whether the benefits are useful to users, and whether any potential benefits are still waiting to be produced by the collaboration. This perspective emphasizes the organizations and actors represented in the collaborating group rather than the group itself. Because all potential collaboration beneficiaries are unlikely to be represented in the collaborating group, approaching representatives of organizations with similar or related mandates outside the collaborating group itself will also be necessary.

		Demand: Do users recognize benefits from the collaboration? (User's assessments)	
		Yes	No
Supply: Do providers think they produce useful benefits? (Providers' assessments)	No	Users recognize benefits not recognized by the providers	Collaboration not useful
	Yes	Collaboration highly useful	Benefits produced not recognized by users

Figure 1. The Provider-User Matrix produces a provider-user perspective of the benefits of collaboration.

When discussing useful science and analyzing the science-policy interface, Sarewitz and Pielke (2007) used a basic supply-demand model to illustrate what constitutes useful research. Distinguishing between researchers' and policymakers' assessments enabled more holistic evaluation of the usefulness of various research projects. To examine the benefits of collaboration, we have developed a provider-user matrix, inspired by Sarewitz and Pielke (2007), that distinguishes between the providers' and users' own assessments of the benefits of collaboration (Figure 1). The matrix describes the provider's assessment of what they regard as the main benefits of the collaborative activity examined. Potential users, here understood as the actors mandated to address issues related to the mandate of the collaborative activity in the same geographical location, are then studied to assess whether or not they have benefited from the benefits identified. The potential users are also evaluated based on their assessment of what benefits would facilitate their specific mandate(s) or task(s). By combining these two dimensions, collaboration benefits can be classified into four categories, raising important issues about the benefits from a broader perspective.

The upper right quadrant indicates that collaboration agendas or capabilities poorly match the needs and expectations of users outside of the collaboration group itself. The upper left and the lower right quadrants indicate missed opportunities, and that there is a high potential to raise the collaboration efficiency. This can be done by better matching provided and expected benefits or by better information exchange between the collaboration groups and the potential users. In the upper left quadrant the users may identify potential benefits that go beyond the collaboration's capabilities or agenda, or, the users actually make use of information or other benefits from the collaboration which the providers themselves do not recognize as useful. Both cases, especially the first, indicate that collaboration efficiency can be raised, for example, by adjusting the collaboration agenda to the needs, or by making the providers more aware of the usefulness of the benefits they produce. The lower right quadrant indicates that the benefits produced are not effectively utilized by the users. One reason may be that the benefits produced are confined within the collaboration group itself. Another reason could be that the benefits produced do not match the needs of the users. A third reason could be that the benefits produced are in fact utilized by the users without them knowing the origin of the benefits. In this case the efficiency of the collaboration can be comparatively high. Finally, the lower left quadrant shows a good match between providers and users assessments of benefits which indicate a high efficiency from a provider-user perspective. The collaboration produces benefits that the users expect and utilize.

Illustrating the Provider-User Matrix: the Ljusnan River Group, Sweden

To further explain the Provider-User Matrix we use a case-study: the Ljusnan River Group (LRG), established to handle flood risk issues. The case is useful for illustrating the matrix because it represents a typical situation where collaboration is seen as key; taking place in a polycentric governance landscape, the issue of flood risk management requires a broad range of expert and practical knowledge, including large uncertainties. The case includes sectors such as crisis and emergency, planning, infrastructure and the environment and both private and public actors at local, regional and super-regional levels which adhere to different mandates, legislations, among others.[2]

The Ljusnan River Group case

The Ljusnan River, located in rural mid-Sweden, is heavily used for hydropower production. The catchment is almost 20,000 km^2 and its most populated municipalities are Bollnäs (approximately 26,000) and Söderhamn (approximately 25,000). The LRG, established in 1996, is one of Sweden's approximately 30 river groups – actor networks involved in governing high flows and their effects. The river groups have no formal obligations but are mandated to disseminate knowledge about the water course among their member organizations and to establish networks to facilitate collaboration during high flows. River groups generally comprise water regulation companies, hydropower producers, county administrative boards (the conveners), municipalities, and central authorities such as the Swedish Civil Contingencies Agency (MSB) and the Swedish Transport Administration.

To explain the case, it is necessary to describe the institutional context of water and flood risk management. Sweden is characterized by strongly decentralized planning, and frequent references to 'the municipalities' planning monopoly' in recent research (e.g., Storbjörk & Hjerpe, 2014) indicate the degree of municipal autonomy as prescribed in the Planning and Building Act (SFS, 2010). Accordingly, the main actors in the Swedish institutional system are the approximately 300 local municipalities. Concerning flooding, the municipalities are responsible for both preventive planning and crisis management. Concerning water resource issues, municipalities are responsible for long-term planning, drinking water supply, wastewater treatment, and environmental protection.

In the last decade, two important EU directives for water and flood risk management have been implemented in Sweden and all EU member states, that is, the Water Framework Directive (WFD; EU, 2000) and the Floods Directive (FD; EU, 2007). The Swedish implementation model has left the municipalities without direct formal obligations from these directives. Instead, parallel and overlapping institutional systems for water and flood risk management have been set up, and important mandates have been given to regional, super-regional, and national authorities that previously had mainly monitoring and supporting roles (SFS, 2009, 2004). These EU directives have challenged the previous institutional system and left it highly complex and fragmented: it is now characterized by many formal actors operating at different and inconsistent geographical scales, steered by different pieces of legislation, and based on different strategies for legitimization (Hedelin, 2005; Lundqvist, 2004; Thorsteinsson, Semadeni-Davies, & Larsson, 2007). For example, the WFD and the FD systems are based on expert decision-making, while the municipal system is based on representative decision-making by locally elected politicians.

To compensate for the heavy expert representation in the WFD system, the WFD implementation strategy in Sweden includes the rapid development of a new type of stakeholder group for water quality issues, the so-called water councils, currently numbering approximately 30. These are catchment-based groups somewhat analogous to the river groups, which have no formal role, but are supported and used as sounding boards by the water district authorities. The water councils generally include a broader range of stakeholders and have a broader mandate than do the river groups, as they are consultation bodies for the water district authorities and are often mandated to involve the public in water environmental issues.

This implies that the studied collaborative arrangement, the LRG, concerns a complementary collaborative arrangement within a context of institutional fragmentation. In this messy context we hypothesize that the Provider-User Matrix would be useful for addressing important issues related to collaboration.

Assessing the benefits in the LRG case

Different approaches and perspectives are used to assess the benefits of collaboration[3] (Leach & Sabatier, 2005; Lubell, 2005). The single case study design used here allows for an in-depth qualitative analysis. To collect data two focus groups (FGs) of providers and users respectively, and five individual semi-structured interviews, were carried out. In total, 14 providers and 13 potential users of the collaborative LRG were interviewed, see Table 1.

FGs have been described as group interviews guided by a moderator using a set of predetermined discussion topics (Morgan, 1998). Using a semi-structured FG approach, similar general, open-ended questions were posed to each group, accompanied by follow-up questions depending on the FG participants' own comments. All members participating in a regular LRG meeting were recruited for the FG discussion; these comprised seven representatives of hydropower companies, four representatives of a municipal rescue services federation, two county administrative board representatives, and one representative of the Swedish National Grid, a state-owned public utility with a mandate to transmit electricity from the major power stations to regional electrical grids (www.svk.se). To form an FG of potential users of the LRG work, representatives of the rescue services, urban planning, and technical services departments from the two most concerned municipalities, Bollnäs and Ovanåker, were invited. The group finally consisted of three

Table 1. Overview of respondents.

Focus group respondents: LRG members, Oct. 2012	Focus group respondents: users in Bollnäs and Ovanåker, Oct. 2012	Individual interview respondents: users, May–Jun. 2013
1. Electricity company, Head of Operation and Maintenance	15. Municipal Federation, Emergency Preparedness	23. Bollnäs Municipality, Technical Services Department, Head
2. National Grid, dam security administrator	16. Municipal Federation, Security Coordinator	24. Bollnäs Municipality, Urban Planning Department
3. County Administrative Board, River Inspection and Rescue Services	17. Municipal Federation, Rescue Services	25. Ovanåker Municipality, Urban Planning and Technical Services, Head
4. Municipal Federation, Rescue Services	18. Bollnäs Municipality, Urban Planning Department, Buildings	26. County Administrative Board, Environmental Analysis Department, Gävleborg
5. The Water Regulation Companies, Water Management	19. Bollnäs Municipality, Urban Planning Department, Buildings	27. Ljusnan River Water Council, Chairperson
6. The Water Regulation Companies, Head of Operation and Maintenance	20. Bollnäs Municipality, Urban Planning Department	
7. Electricity Company, Water Regulation	21. Bollnäs Municipality, Technical Services Department	
8. Electricity Company, Head of Operations	22. Ovanåker Municipality, Technical Services Department	
9. County Administrative Board, Extreme Events		
10. Municipal Federation, Head of Rescue Services		
11. Electricity Company, Head of Production		
12. Municipal Federation, Head of Rescue Services		
13. Municipal Federation, Head		
14. Electricity Company, Planning		

representatives of the Municipal Federation (i.e., Emergency Preparedness, Security Coordination, and Rescue Services), four representatives of Bollnäs Municipality (i.e., Urban Planning and Technical Services), and one representative of Ovanåker Municipality (i.e., Technical Services). To broaden the scope of potential users, five complementary individual interviews were conducted with heads of the Urban Planning and Technical Services departments of Bollnäs and Ovanåker Municipalities and with key potential users engaged in WFD work. All respondents had direct or indirect responsibility for managing high flows or their effects as part of their work assignments. The individual interview guide contained open-ended questions about present activities and challenges concerning high flows, current actor collaborations, knowledge of the LRG, and actual and potential benefits of the LRG.

All interviews were audio-recorded and transcribed verbatim. The focus groups lasted two hours and the individual interviews 30–60 minutes. The analysis consisted of coding and looking for trends and recurrent themes to concentrate meanings (Marková, Linell, Grossen, & Orvig, 2007). The transcripts were treated separately and the contents of each respondent's or FG participant's contributions were examined in detail. Subsequently, patterns were distinguished and meanings categorized in accordance with our research questions concerning respondents' understandings of the benefits of collaboration. Various recurring benefit categories featuring in the material were identified (Kvale, 1997). The FG episodes and interview excerpts were compiled and structured in terms of particular benefit categories. Those excerpts and episodes with a particular bearing on the benefits of collaboration were highlighted for more thorough analysis. When present-ing our empirical results, respondent statements and reflections are emphasized, combin-ing individual viewpoints with more general patterns. Although allowing interpretations based on individual statements – where the analysis reflects individual views, perspec-tives, and experiences – we attempt to increase the validity of our interpretations by comparing statements from different interviews (Silverman, 1993). Benefit categories identified by providers and users were compared to identify gaps that collaboration could potentially fill. The numbers in brackets refer to respondents in Table 1.

Provider-assessed benefits

When asked about the benefits of the LRG, provider respondents frequently refer to the situation before the group was established, and in its initial stages. Before the LRG, respondents agree, confrontation and a lack of understanding of other organizations' roles and mandates were the norm. This resulted in destructive repetition of arguments, a focus on who was to blame, and weak outcomes of crisis management exercises involving many actors. As one respondent recalls:

> Before the establishment [of the LRG] there was more confrontation between rescue services and electricity companies [...] before we used to blame [...] it was the electricity companies who were to blame for all floods. [4]

By regularly meeting representatives of other organizations involved in handling high flows in the Ljusnan river (the LRG convenes twice per year, once via telephone and once face to face), group members have gained a better understanding of the mandates of the other organizations. Gaining a more thorough understanding of others' roles and man-dates, one respondent argues, is a prerequisite for success in the LRG [9], not only by establishing trust but also by better understanding the intricacies of agency and authority in the institutionally fragmented flood management regime. One respondent claims that understanding one's role in relation to others' roles in the overall flood management system is a primary benefit of the LRG [2].

Respondents also agree that the LRG has particularly improved trust between the two former antagonists, the electricity companies and emergency services. Trust forms the basis for sharing knowledge and water discharge data. The electricity companies' daily prognoses, used for regulating power production, are now fed to the municipal rescue services when a high flow situation is emerging. This has improved the municipalities' early warning capacity regarding both high and moderate flows and, accordingly, has enhanced their ability to prevent or reduce damage to infrastructure and buildings. Water discharge data are also fed to the County Administrative Board, which can alert other organizations should a high flow occur, which happens about once a year. In autumn 2011, when an emergency was emerging rapidly, the LRG members shared all available hydrological data, significantly increasing the knowledge bases of several members. The LRG members were consequently able to spread a consistent message when interviewed by the media, without having to coordinate their media messages. This might have contributed to the shift in media coverage from alarmist messages to conveying information about the situation and joining forces with the LRG to cope with the flood. This example, the members acknowledge, demonstrates how the LRG has directly improved the ability to manage high flows and, consequently, reduced the extent of damage to infrastructure and buildings.

Another example of a benefit stemming from improved trust is described by a respondent who is a member of several river collaborating groups. In one group in which several electricity companies are members, the companies started granting other companies access to their facilities [3], which could lead to better self-inspection and improved emergency response. Compared with that of other river groups, respondents contend that the social climate in this group is the best [7].

Over time, a shared group identity has been formed. This is pointed out by all respondents, who claim that both molding a shared and more multi-faceted understanding of the complex socio-ecological flood response system and the mandate of the LRG group have contributed to this identity. By assembling pieces of knowledge about, for example, the hydrological system, water-related infrastructure in cities, and critical societal infrastructure, a more advanced understanding of the flood response system has emerged. This means that the ability of each organization to assess the effectiveness of various flood protection measures and actions has improved. For example, group members are now aware that regulating water flow (i.e., increasing flow through dams) is insufficient to reduce the impact of an extreme weather event. This more advanced understanding is also becoming a shared understanding. Another benefit of the more advanced understanding of the flood response system is the positive outcome of a recent crisis management exercise. The multi-faceted understanding of the flood system also increases the likelihood of being granted funds by the national agency, which requires a river system perspective. Respondents frequently use the terms 'we' and 'our' when referring to the LRG mandates, activities, and outcomes, indicating a shared identity as an LRG member and that a sense of shared ownership has been established (e.g., Bryan, 2004).

Most of the above advantages primarily benefit the organizations represented on the LRG. However, the data also contain examples of benefits that extend beyond the group. For example, one respondent says that, in internal discussions in his own organization and municipality, he has sometimes articulated the perspective of electricity companies to explain why certain situations have occurred [4].

Respondents see three LRG benefits that extend beyond the organizations represented in the collaborating group itself: first, identifying previously unknown risks and sensitive or exposed areas, for example, as done by the dam break inquiry initiated by the LRG, and, second, initiating projects and measures to reduce vulnerability to flooding. These measures are often executed by one or a few LRG organizations. The most elaborate is a dam break pilot project. Other examples include guidelines for locating petrol stations and second homes, and clearing the river course of vegetation and silt. The LRG members also frequently 'brainstorm' in the group before going ahead with projects in their own organizations [9]. Third, organizations mandated to inspect dams see the LRG discussions as part of their inspections: at the LRG meetings, they are continuously informed about the current situation, and the improved trust facilitates the inspection process.

User-assessed benefits

Only one of the 13 user respondents is familiar with the LRG group and its mandates. He works as security coordinator of the Municipal Federation and is familiar with the LRG dam break study. Most respondents have not heard of the LRG at all; some of them possess fragmented information, but often confuse the group with other collaborative arrangements, or did not know of the group's mandate.

According to users' assessments few benefits are obtained from the LRG, and no respondent stated having used information or material emanating from the LRG. The respondents in higher positions generally know who is representing their organization in the LRG, but few have been informed of its benefits. One respondent says:

> [X] is member of the LRG from our side, but he doesn't distribute any information from the group internally, not that I know of anyway. [26]

After being informed about the mandate and members of the LRG, the respondents become more or less enthusiastic, and display an interest in developing connections to the LRG in order to take advantage of its provisions. All agree that important linkages exist between the LRG's mandate and their own organizations. The main provision targeted is the LRG's deeper understanding of the hydrological system. This knowledge is especially emphasized by respondents from the municipal planning and technical departments, who work with technical infrastructure and urban development plans. For example, they believe that this knowledge would contribute to a better understanding of how to manage sensitive parts of the infrastructure, and provide a better knowledge base for planning new urban areas. The LRG could therefore convey the river system perspective, which is difficult to obtain at the municipal level. Such a perspective is important for effective flood risk management, because a measure to protect one population center might have to be taken in an adjacent municipality, because several river system actors might need to cooperate to achieve sufficient funding for a measure, or just because of the need to reach a necessary shared understanding of goals and means. One proposed way to apply the river system perspective of the LRG is to use it as an arena for comprehensive planning of flood reduction measures.

Respondents working on water quality issues at the municipal, regional, and river basin levels agree that the LRG could contribute a river basin perspective, but that this perspective needs to be complemented with environmental concerns in the discussions, plans, and activities pertaining to the governance of high flows. One way to do this would be to broaden participation in the LRG to include people working on the WFD or on water quality issues in the municipalities. As one respondent expresses it:

> I definitely think one should do that [i.e., include water environmental issues] because it is a complex system we are talking about. [22]

Overall, the respondents working on water and environmental issues are more concerned with how the LRG can be broadened to include their interests, while the respondents from the technical and planning areas are more interested in gaining access to the knowledge and perspectives established by the LRG.

The Provider-User Matrix: overlaying providers' and users' assessments

The providers' and users' assessments are now overlaid using the Provider-User Matrix (Figure 2). The upper right quadrant, where both users and providers assess the collaboration as not useful, is not valid in the LRG case. While the users could not account for any utilized benefits from the collaborating group, the providers gave a rich description of benefits that clearly could benefit the users (lower right). Here the matrix shows that linkages should be developed between providers and users in order to reap the benefits. These benefits include identification of sensitive areas, establishment of projects, formulation of guidelines and clearing the water courses. Using the Provider-User Matrix to compare these benefits with the mandates and main challenges cited by the users indicates that several benefits fall within their mandates and, thus, are potentially beneficial for the user. For example, the urban planners requested better scenarios for areas exposed to flooding when they are planning new areas. Interestingly, the users also suggested that the LRG could benefit from gaining access to more advanced knowledge of infrastructure and activities in the exposed areas produced by the users' organizations. The matrix here indicates that also the providers would benefit from more linkages and the linkage should be bidirectional. Respondents mandated with water quality or environmental conservation tasks claimed that clearing the water course even counteracted their tasks, causing negative environmental effects. By linking to this user, the LRG understanding of the river system would be challenged and could, potentially lead to more holistic understanding of it. Hence, one way to make the benefits provided by the LRG more useful could be to involve potential users more actively, and to make them aware of the LRG benefits produced. Doing so, however, does not lie within the current LRG mandate. This illustrates that the Provider-User Matrix could not only be used to identify recommendations for improved collaboration but also deepens the understanding of the different contexts, facilitating identification of relevant recommendations with high legitimacy in the local context.

The upper-left quadrant describes the benefits the users perceive but that the LRG members currently fail to recognize as useful for the users. The Provider-User Matrix demonstrates that these benefits stay with the providers, even if users could benefit from them. These benefits are, particularly, access to better hydrological data that are currently unavailable to them, access to the river basin perspective produced by the collaboration, and more integrated flood risk management, which the users cannot access. This means that the LRG members have not realized the full potential of the benefits provided by their collaboration. Here dissemination and communication are key. Communication, however, does not lie within the current LRG mandate. When the LRG members share hydrological

| | | Demand: Do users recognize benefits from the collaboration? (User's assessments) | |
		Yes	No
Supply: Do providers think they produce useful benefits?	**No**	Benefits recognized by users but not by providers: – access to better data – access to river basin perspective – more integrated flood risk management	Not valid in the LRG case
(Providers' assessments)	**Yes**	No benefits explicitly identified by both providers and users Implicitly, rescue services have access to more data; the crisis preparedness has increased, projects have been developed, and the river has been cleared.	Benefits produced not recognized by users: – exposed areas identified – project established – guidelines developed – clearing the water course – LRG members share their knowledge in their organizations

Figure 2.   Benefits of the LRG collaboration identified by providers and users.

data, all of them benefit from enhanced awareness of when and how to respond to high flows. This has particularly benefited data-poor organizations, such as the rescue services. The transcripts suggest that hydrological data are shared mainly with LRG members and, hence, that the benefits have so far been confined to LRG member organizations. These hydrological data could potentially benefit other users, if the LRG members agree to share them with the wider user community. While these observations do not rule out that other officials may have used the data, the general unawareness of the LRG suggests room to improve the dissemination of data. Furthermore, the LRG has constructed a model of the river basin, facilitating understanding from that perspective. Organizations operating at a smaller geographical scale would particularly benefit from greater familiarity with the river basin perspective, because it would enable the evaluation of any measures from a broadened perspective and permit more coordinated action. This leads us to the third benefit category that users regard as useful, namely, more integrated flood risk management. By gaining access to an enhanced understanding of the roles and mandates that clarify agency and establish inter-organizational trust, which emanate from the LRG collaboration, other organizations would be better able to see their own mandates in relation to the overall picture.

Even as the study failed to establish any utilized benefits that were explicitly recognized by both users and providers (lower-left), collaboration was beneficial for the group members themselves, who bring back new knowledge to their own organization. By matching benefits identified in the provider interviews with the responses of potential users, this study suggests that the rescue services have benefited from better access to hydrological data, and that the rescue services and other organizations participating in crisis management have likely benefited from a more holistic understanding of the flood regime and of how different actors' mandates shape agency, leading to a more favorable outcome in a crisis management exercise. Their organizations also likely benefited from the projects developed and from the river clearing. Interviews suggest that inducing benefits in their own organizations could be improved if the group membership became less tied to an individual and strongly tied to specific functions and departments. This could also be achieved by instructing and providing resources to LRG members to communicate internally (Figure 2).

Although the provider assessments show that the LRG collaboration does provide a number of important benefits, the Provider-User Matrix reveals that there is still a large potential to develop the LRG collaboration. This is also supported by the user respondents' claim that collaborative forums are vital in the polycentric Swedish water management regime.

Discussion and conclusions

The Provider-User Matrix demonstrates the merits of widening the picture

The application of the Provider-User Matrix to the LRG case well demonstrates the merit of widening the picture by also including potential users of the studied collaboration. By doing so we were able to identify different views on provider-identified benefits and benefits that were only identified by users. This resulted in a more comprehensive view of the usefulness of the collaboration compared to using the collaborating group as the only empirical basis. This observation is in line with results from previous studies that put collaboration in relation to its context (Campbell et al., 2011; Hardy & Koontz, 2009; Koontz, 2005; Weber, 2003) and supports the argument that broader approaches are important with regard to issues of benefits and utility of collaboration. In the LRG case, the providers identified a much larger range of benefits than the users did, who could, in fact, not recall utilizing any of those benefits. Also, the users identified several additional benefits that they could potentially utilize, some of which the LRG collaborative did not identify themselves.

A wider picture should not be conflated with a complete picture

It is important to note, however, that although the Provider-User Matrix allows for a more comprehensive assessment compared to collaboration-group-only approaches, the proposed matrix does not cover all aspects of benefits. For example, in the LRG case, as pointed out above, some of the benefits stressed by the providers but not by the users have probably benefited the users, such as access to more data, the crisis exercise and the clearing of the river. The Provider-User Matrix provides the estimates of the collaboration group and of the users examined, and it is these perspectives and their combination that the matrix can describe. There may well be benefits produced that fall outside the lenses of the examined groups, and, as argued in the introduction, a benefit identified even by both the targeted groups could be seen as a non-benefit from an opposite perspective (e.g., opposed interests to restrict building in flood-prone areas as the interest to attract new inhabitants in rural areas by offering near-shore housing). Like all approaches to study benefit, it is important to keep in mind that the issue of benefit can never be disconnected from values. The more perspectives included, however, the more full covering the assessment.

The Provider-User Matrix could be used to demonstrate general patterns

We have illustrated the Provider-User Matrix by a single case study. This is not meant to limit the use of the matrix to qualitative study designs. Another, quite different, way of utilizing the Provider-User Matrix could be through a series of quantitative surveys targeted at providers and users in a large number of collaborations. We believe that quantitative approaches would be useful in relation to the Provider-User Matrix if the aim is to study general patterns of, for example, the relationship between providers' and users' assessment of benefits. A way to adopt the matrix for such study designs could be to use specific and categorized benefits as a basis for the survey. Possible ways to categorize benefits are as outputs, outcomes and products, direct and indirect benefits, physical and institutional, and so on. See Koontz and Thomas (2006) for explanation of different categories.

Ensuring benefits reach their users

While the Provider-User Matrix has the ability to provide a more holistic picture of collaboration benefits, the matrix also sheds light over mismatches – between provided and needed benefits, and between provided and utilized benefits. This, we argue, shows that the matrix also can be a tool for making collaboration more efficient and useful. Applying the Provider-User Matrix to the LRG case revealed possible ways of making better use of the provided benefits and to establish the potential benefits identified by the users. For example, the advanced understanding of the river hydraulics developed by the LRG could become more useful if knowledge of the LRG's role and mandate were spread among potential users and if well thought out structures and processes were established for linking the LRG and the user organizations. This would also allow for operationalizing the potential benefits identified by some of the users, such as access to the river basin perspective in municipal flood risk planning and more integrated water and flood risk management. Expanding the scope of the issues handled by the collaboration has shown to be valuable in other cases where collaboration has been studied in relation to its context (Koontz, 2005).

But applying the Provider-User Matrix does not only provide a knowledge basis in relation to the studied collaboration; it can also be a way to start developing the collaboration further. Our interviews informed the users about the LRG and its mandate. Most users expressed enthusiasm and an interest to take part or make better use of the benefits it provided. For example, one user argued: 'I will talk to the person here who is now responsible for the work on the Water Framework Directive and to [X] about the connections between the WFD work and the LRG's work, so that we can take advantage of them properly' [26]. Based on this observation, we believe that in addition to a research approach, it would be interesting to study the use of the matrix in practice, as a tool for collaboration designers. Effective ways of establishing and developing collaborations are inherently context dependent (Koontz & Thomas, 2006), and, as illustrated here, the Provider-User Matrix supports a systematic approach towards such context-specific knowledge, and to the formulation of context-specific recommendations.

To conclude, our paper has introduced the Provider-User Matrix that can provide important insights into the benefits of collaborative arrangements, which is a common feature of polycentric governance. These insights, and the process of developing them, indicate that the Provider-User Matrix can serve as a tool for both understanding collaboration arrangements and increasing their efficiency. Also, since our case study supports the argument made in the introduction, we hope this study will inspire further research attempts to apply broadened and contextual perspectives on collaboration.

Notes

1. The collaboration providers are here defined as the individual members of the collaborating network or group itself. By users we mean the organizations and actors represented in the collaborating group rather than the group itself. Because all potential collaboration beneficiaries are unlikely to be represented in the collaborating group, actors with similar or related mandates outside the collaborating group are also defined as users here.
2. The case is used as a means for explaining the Provider-User Matrix. The case is not intended to generalize what benefits collaboration has or the relationship between provider and user perspectives.
3. Many of these approaches are quantitative (e.g., questionnaires, numbers of projects completed) and intend to provide a general picture of the level of success or the kinds of benefits that collaboration can deliver. For the purpose of explaining the Provider-User Matrix we use a single case study design which enables in-depth interviews with providers and users and context-specific understanding. This is intended to illustrate the matrix's potential to deliver a deeper understanding of the collaboration and the way it could be developed, as well as of how it is related to contextual factors.

References

Agger, A., & Lofgren, K. (2008). Democratic assessment of collaborative planning processes. *Planning Theory, 7*, 145–164. doi:10.1177/1473095208090432

Andonova, L B., Betsill, M M., & Bulkeley, H. (2009). Transnational climate governance. *Global Environmental Politics, 9*, 52–73. doi:10.1162/glep.2009.9.2.52

Ansell, C., & Gash, A. (2008). Collaborative governance in theory and practice. *Journal of Public Administration Research Theory, 18*, 543–571. doi:10.1093/jopart/mum032

Bryan, T. A. (2004). Tragedy averted: The promise of collaboration. *Society and Natural Resources, 17*, 881–896. doi:10.1080/08941920490505284

Campbell, J. T., Koontz, T. M., & Bonnell, J. E. (2011). Does collaboration promote grass-roots behavior change? Farmer adoption of best management practices in two watersheds. *Society & Natural Resources, 24*, 1127–1141. doi:10.1080/08941920.2010.512358

Conley, A., & Moote, M. A. (2003). Evaluating collaborative natural resource management. *Society and Natural Resources, 16*, 371–386. doi:10.1080/08941920309181

EU. (2000). Directive of the European parliament and of the council establishing a framework for community action in the field of water policy (2000/60/EC). *Official Journal, L327*.

EU. (2007). Directive of the European parliament and of the council on the assessment and management of flood risks (2007/60/EC). *Official Journal, L288*.

Habermas, J. (1984). *The theory of communicative action volume 1: Reason and the rationalization of society*. Cambridge: Polity Press.

Hardy, S. D., & Koontz, T. M. (2009). Rules for collaboration: Institutional analysis of group membership and levels of action in watershed partnerships. *Policy Studies Journal, 37*, 393–414. doi:10.1111/j.1541-0072.2009.00320.x

Healey, P. (1997). *Collaborative planning: Shaping places in fragmenting societies*. London: MacMillan.

Hedelin, B. (2005). Potential implications of the EU water framework directive in Sweden. *European Journal of Spatial Development, 14*.

Hedelin, B. (2007). Criteria for the assessment of sustainable water management. *Environmental Management, 39*, 151–163. doi:10.1007/s00267-004-0387-0

Koontz, T. M. (2005). We finished the plan, so now what? Impacts of collaborative stakeholder participation on land use policy. *Policy Studies Journal, 33*, 459–481. doi:10.1111/j.1541-0072.2005.00125.x

Koontz, T. M., & Thomas, C. W. (2006). What do we know and need to know about the environmental outcomes of collaborative management? *Public Administration Review, 66*, 111–121. doi:10.1111/j.1540-6210.2006.00671.x

Kvale, S. (1997). *Den kvalitativa forskningsintervjun*. Lund: Studentlitteratur. [In Swedish].

Leach, W. D. (2002). Surveying diverse stakeholder groups. *Society & Natural Resources, 15*, 641–649. doi:10.1080/08941920290069245

Leach, W. D., & Pelkey, N. W. (2001). Making watershed partnerships work: A review of the empirical literature. *Journal of Water Resources Planning and Management, 127*, 378–385. doi:10.1061/(ASCE)0733-9496(2001)127:6(378)

Leach, W. D., Pelkey, N. W., & Sabatier, P. A. (2002). Stakeholder partnerships as collaborative policymaking: Evaluation criteria applied to watershed management in California and Washington. *Journal of Policy Analysis and Management, 21*, 645–670. doi:10.1002/pam.10079

Leach, W. D., & Sabatier, P. (2005). Are trust and social capital the keys to success? Watershed partnerships in California and Washington. In P. Sabatier, W. Focht, M. Lubell, Z. Trachtenberg, A. Vedlitz, & M. Matlock (Eds.), *Swimming upstream: Collaborative approaches to watershed management* (pp. 231–258). Cambridge, MA: MIT.

Lubell, M. (2005). Do watershed partnerships enhance beliefs conducive to collective action? In P. Sabatier, W. Focht, M. Lubell, Z. Trachtenberg, A. Vedlitz & M. Matlock (Eds.), *Swimming upstream: Collaborative approaches to watershed management* (pp. 201–232). Cambridge, MA: MIT.

Lundqvist, L. (2004). Integrating Swedish water resource management: A multi-level governance trilemma. *Local Esnvironment, 9*, 413–424. doi:10.1080/1354983042000255324

Margerum, R. D. (1999). Profile: Integrated environmental management: The foundations for successful practice. *Environmental Management, 24*, 151–166. doi:10.1007/s002679900223

Margerum, R. D. (2011). *Beyond consensus: Improving collaborative planning and management*. Cambridge: MIT Press.

Marková, I., Linell, P., Grossen, M., & Orvig, A. S. (2007). *Dialogue in focus groups: Exploring socially shared knowledge*. London: Equinox.

Montin, S. (2000). Between fragmentation and co-ordination: The changing role of local government in Sweden. *Public Management, 2*(1), 1–23. doi:10.1080/146166700360136

Morgan, D. L. (1998). *Planning focus groups*. Thousand Oaks, CA: SAGE Publications.

Ostrom, E. (1990). *Governing the commons: The evolution of institutions for collective action*. Cambridge: Cambridge University Press.

Pagdee, A., Kim, Y-S., & Daugherty, P. J. (2006). What makes community forest management successful: A meta-study from community forests throughout the world. *Society & Natural Resources, 19*(1), 33–52. doi:10.1080/08941920500323260

Pahl-Wostl, C., Craps, M., Dewulf, A., Mostert, E., Tabara, D., & Taillieu, T. (2007). Social learning and water resources management. *Ecology and Society, 12*, 5.

Sarewitz, D., & Pielke Jr, R. A. (2007). The neglected heart of science policy: Reconciling supply of and demand for science. *Environmental Science and Policy, 10*, 5–16. doi:10.1016/j.envsci.2006.10.001

Schuett, M. A., Selin, S. W., & Carr, D. S. (2001). Making it work: Keys to successful collaboration in natural resource management. *Environmental Management, 27*, 587–593. doi:10.1007/s002670010172

SFS. (2004). *Ordinance on water quality administration (2004:660)*. Stockholm: Swedish government.

SFS. (2009). *Flood risk ordinance (2009:956)*. Stockholm: Swedish government.

SFS. (2010). *Planning and building act (2010:900)*. Stockholm: Swedish government.

Silverman, D. (1993). *Interpreting qualitative data: Methods for analyzing talk, text and interaction*. London: Sage.

Storbjörk, S., & Hjerpe, M. (2014). Sometimes climate adaptation is politically correct: A case study of planners and politicians negotiating climate adaptation in waterfront spatial planning. *European Planning Studies, 22*(11), 2268–2286. doi:10.1080/09654313.2013.830697

Thorsteinsson, D., Semadeni-Davies, A. S., & Larsson, R. (2007). Planning for river induced floods in urban areas: Experiences and key issues for Sweden. *Flood Risk Management in Europe, 25*, 485–503. doi:10.1007/978-1-4020-4200-3_25

Weber, E. P. (2003). *Bringing society back in: Grassroots ecosystem management, accountability, and sustainable communities*. Cambridge: MIT Press.

Adapting to catastrophic water scarcity in agriculture through social networking and inter-generational occupational transitioning

Ram Ranjan

Faculty of Science, Macquarie University, Sydney, NSW, Australia

Increasing frequency of drought threatens the long-term viability of agriculture in many regions of the world. Some farmers will exit the agricultural industry abruptly, but for many, the path out of agriculture is prolonged and involves several generations within a household. This paper presents a model of dynamic inter-generational preferences and occupational choices to explore possible transition paths out of agriculture. Differing preferences across generations within a farming household are incorporated through a dynamically-evolving utility function, which influences the time paths of optimal investments in human, social and natural capital. A dwindling natural resource base, such as groundwater, requires increasing reliance on urban livelihoods. However, inter-generational differences in preferences for rural versus urban lifestyles, modelled as different weights in the household's utility function, may determine whether this occupational transition can be attained.

Introduction

Climate change is causing an increase in the frequency of drought (Rodell, Velicogna, & Famiglietti, 2009; Taylor et al., 2012; Trenberth et al., 2014). More frequent, severe, or prolonged drought poses existential challenges to farming communities around the world. For subsistence farming households, consequences may include reductions in food security, drinking water access, household income, and ability to repay debt (Harvey et al., 2014; Hazell & Hess, 2010; Ye et al., 2012). Coping mechanisms may include sending household members to neighboring regions or countries to work, sending children to live with relatives in urban areas, liquidating livestock, or reducing the size or number of meals eaten per day (Morton, 2007; Roncoli, Ingram, & Kirshen, 2001). In extreme cases, the impact of water scarcity has been even more disastrous. For example, drought has been implicated in a 15% increase in the relative risk of suicide among rural males, ages 30–49 years, in New South Wales, Australia (Hanigan, Butler, Kokic, & Hutchinson, 2012). Anecdotal evidence for this link between drought and suicide also exists in some rural areas of India (Nagaraj, 2008).

Government response to such droughts has varied widely across countries. In some countries, such as Australia, farming exit programs have been introduced (Department of Agriculture, Fisheries and Forestry [DAFF], 2012). Under some of these programs, farmers who were significantly drought-hit and met other eligibility criteria were offered 150,000 Australian dollars to exit farming and sell their farm property. In the US, groundwater levels have played an important role in determining privately whether farmers exit agriculture or not (Schuck, Frasier, Webb, Ellingson, & Umberger, 2005). In developing countries, such as India, watershed management plans have existed for a considerable time in response to prolonged water scarcity (Kerr, Pangare, & Panagre, 2002). Watershed programs, in contrast to farm exit programs, aim to mitigate ground-water scarcity by building check-dams that enhance groundwater infiltration. Unfortunately, their impact has not been significant, especially from an equity perspective (Kerr et al., 2002). Another program in India, the Mahatma Gandhi National Rural Employment Guarantee Act (MGNREGA), guarantees one hundred days of employment in the manual unskilled sector to every rural household (Government of India, 2012). By providing employment during drought periods, such programs help alleviate hardship in the short-run. However, managing long-term declines in water availability is a different challenge, both for governments and farming households.

Prolonged water scarcity in agriculture, due in part to climate change, raises key questions about whether and how the most vulnerable farming households can smoothly transition out of agriculture. Given that exit assistance is neither available to everyone nor available indefinitely, what are optimal long-term exit strategies for households that face natural resource constraints and have differing occupational capabilities? Furthermore, how do farmers accumulate and substitute between different forms of capital – natural, social, and human – to facilitate a successful exit and secure alternative long-term sources of income?

When farmers' livelihoods are threatened by depletion of key natural resources, such as groundwater, they are forced to adapt in the short-run while simultaneously developing and implementing a long-run plan to exit agriculture. In extreme cases, the most vulnerable farmers may be forced to exit abruptly. For most farmers, however, exiting is a process that involves and affects multiple generations. The oldest generation (e.g., those in the over 50 years age-group) may find it impractical to exit farming, even when it becomes unsustainable, due to limited opportunities for career switches or an attachment to the farming lifestyle. The middle generation (e.g., the age-group between 30 and 50 years), within the same household, may have more options but might be constrained in their choices by a need to ensure their children's education is not disrupted by sudden migration or income fluctuation. Their preferences might also be influenced by those of the older generation. This effectively constrains their set of possible livelihood-related actions. Finally, the youngest generation (e.g., up to 30 years of age), may still be educating themselves and generally have the highest potential for attaining careers outside of agriculture, if they choose to do so. Evidence from several developing countries, such as China, India, Nepal and Vietnam, suggests that younger generations prefer to exit farming, even in the absence of recurring drought (Emran & Shilpi, 2011; Emran & Sun, 2011). For farming households that rely primarily on family labor, lack of participation in agriculture by future generations could impose new constraints and challenges.

Multi-generational differences in opportunities and preferences, within the same farming household, creates complex tradeoffs which need to be carefully managed during transition planning, especially when increasing water scarcity makes the future viability of agriculture even more uncertain. Ensuring that the youngest generation makes a smooth transition out of agriculture into other formal or informal sectors of the economy may require an intensive focus on human capital accumulation (i.e., education). The role of educational attainment and human capital accumulation in this transition has been widely researched (e.g., Emran & Shilpi, 2011; Emran & Sun, 2011; also see Becker & Tomes, 1979 for early seminal work on inter-generational mobility). Human capital accumulation may challenge the household's existing management plans, as the need for financial wealth to support human capital accumulation strains natural capital stocks, such as groundwater. More frequent droughts, due to climate-change, would only exacerbate this strain.

Gains in human capital accumulation at the expense of natural capital may, in turn, affect the dynamics of social networks (or social network capital) in agriculture. Social network capital is known to enhance agricultural productivity. However, reduced groundwater reservoirs might cause conflicts between groundwater users and lead to an erosion of social capital. Such erosion would hasten the decline in productivity of a farmer who already faces a binding natural resource constraint (Fafchamps & Minten, 2002; Hartman & Arata, 2011; Krishna & Uphoff, 1999; Putnam, 1993, 1995, 2014).

Models that incorporate inter-generational decision making are not new to the economics literature. Multiple or overlapping generations models abound in macroeconomic studies (e.g., Azariadis, 1993). There have also been some applications in the environmental economics literature. For instance, Antoci (2009) argues that when environmental degradation leads to self-protection through increased private consumption, it also affects multiple generations by exacerbating existing environmental problems through the production of polluting goods.

Direct applications of multi-generational models in agriculture are hard to find, especially in the context of prolonged water scarcity. Most studies of drought are dedicated to modelling farmers' adaptation through water markets, water trading, or technology adoption (e.g., Carey & Zilberman, 2002; Khanna, Epohue, & Hornbaker, 1999; Zilberman et al., 1995). An emerging body of literature is dedicated to modelling farmers' resilience to climate-change-induced droughts (e.g., Peck & Adams, 2012; Ranjan & Athalye, 2009; Ranjan, 2013). However, increased frequency of droughts observed in several parts of the world in recent decades has created a need to study how farmers' agricultural choices may affect livelihood opportunities for future generations within the same household. Complex inter-generational tradeoffs arise when farming households attempt to plan an optimally-timed exit from agriculture. Although abrupt exits from agriculture draw policymakers' attention, less-visible long-term exits are also complicated and stressful for farming households.

This paper addresses how such inter-generational choices are made, in light of long-term declines in water availability, and what implications they have for future generations' livelihoods and the household's well-being. A stylized model is developed to explore the roles of three generations within a farming household in the planning of a smooth occupational transition out of agriculture. One of the key features of the model is that it allows for a gradual occupational shift rather than an abrupt exit, in response to prolonged drought. This gradual shift involves long-term planning and reliance upon (and substitution between) various forms of capital, specifically natural, social, and human. To incorporate preferences for an agricultural way of life, as well as for social and human capital accumulation, the model includes them directly in the utility function. Although traditional economic models typically incorporate human capital in the household's budget constraint, alternative approaches exist. Finkelstein et al. (2013) includes health – a form of human capital – as an argument in the utility function, along with consumption. Their argument is that marginal utility of consumption is lower for an ill person than for a healthy person. Similarly, Löffler (2001) assumes wealth-dependent utility functions, rather than just wealth-constrained decision making.

Groundwater scarcity and the risk of its irreversible loss is incorporated in the model to evaluate natural resource conditions under which human capital accumulation may or may not be feasible for the household. Since human capital accumulation is crucial for transitioning out of agriculture (Huffman, 2001; Taylor & Martin, 2001), factors that support or impede it are considered. In particular, the role of inter-generational differences in preferences over the accumulation of certain capital types is incorporated in a household decision making model. The role of differing rates of time discounting among the three generations is also explored.

This paper makes a number of key contributions to the existing literature. It develops a model that explores long-term adaptation to prolonged water scarcity in agriculture through inter-generational shifts in occupational choices. The model also incorporates differing preferences of generations within the same household to realistically capture tradeoffs that may arise within the household's decision making process. Finally, the paper models social networking as an activity undertaken by one generation to not only enhance agricultural productivity but also to indirectly help the next generation accumulate human capital (i.e., education). To the best of my knowledge, social networking models in which one generation takes up networking to benefit the next generation have not previously been developed in the literature.

The paper proceeds by providing a model outline, then a more-detailed description of the dynamic optimization model, followed by insights from a numerical example, and conclusions.

1. Model outline

Consider a farming household that derives its utility primarily from consumption, but also holds preferences for accumulating different types of capital. These types of capital may be associated with a particular lifestyle choice of a specific generation within the household. For instance, a healthy stock of natural capital, which is represented by groundwater here, ensures a successful agricultural lifestyle such that the family does not need to migrate in the future. Similarly, if the youngest generation within the household acquires human capital (i.e., education), they might be able to find employment outside of agriculture and lead a more comfortable life. Assuming the household has at least three different generations within it, financial resource constraints may put the lifestyle ambitions of one generation at loggerheads with another. Water scarcity could exacerbate the challenge of achieving a smooth occupational transition by reducing crop income and creating tradeoffs between consumption and education.

Preferences of the household for different capital types may shift over time as one generation becomes older and the next generation takes over. More formally, this inter-generational shift in preferences is incorporated in the model by assuming that each generation differs in the weights they place on various components of the household utility function. The household's utility function comprises consumption and various forms of capital, and is specified as:

$$U(t) = U[\phi \cdot c(t), \{1 - \phi - \tau_1(t) - \tau_2(t)\} \cdot g(t), \{\tau_1(t) + \tau_2(t)\} \cdot h(t)], \qquad (1)$$

where parameters $\tau_1(t) + \tau_2(t)$ are the weights placed on human capital $h(t)$; φ is the weight placed on consumption $c(t)$, and $\{1 - \varphi - \tau_1(t) - \tau_2(t)\}$ is the weight placed on groundwater $g(t)$. The weights $\tau_1(t)$ and $\tau_2(t)$ are dynamic and evolve over time (see Bisin & Verdier, 2001 for applications of dynamic preferences in the context of cultural transmission). The sum of weights placed on all arguments of the utility function is never to exceed one. Over time, as the weights placed on human capital increase, the weights on agricultural lifestyle decline. The variable $g(t)$ also serves as a proxy for agricultural lifestyle. Since farm production is assumed to be mostly groundwater-dependent, a depletion of groundwater makes farming increasingly unviable and hence threatens the agricultural lifestyle.

The household's utility function sees a change in its weights after a certain period of time, owing to changes in the ages (and hence leadership roles) of household members. For instance, the oldest generation's preferences may carry a bigger weight in the beginning (e.g., the first 10 to 20 years), after which time the middle generation's preferences become dominant for another 10 to 20 years, until the newest generation's preferences take over. I assume here that the oldest generation places a relatively higher weight on natural capital (groundwater) in the household's utility function, because it ensures a prolonged agricultural lifestyle. The middle generation may be forced to alter this weighting by placing higher weights on the human capital of the youngest generation, which comes at the cost of lower weights on natural capital. The youngest generation eventually alters these weights in favor of human capital. It is important to emphasize here that the decision making body comprises all three generations of the household, who maximize overall utility across time. The assumption that weights on the arguments in the utility function are dynamic reflects the fact that, as time passes, household preferences shift away from natural capital and towards human capital. This assumption also draws support from collective household models used in the microeconomics literature, wherein several decision makers within a household, who vary in their preferences, cooperatively interact to optimize their household utility function (e.g., Vermeulen, 2002).

2. Model

Assume the representative farming household produces a composite agricultural commodity using only water $w(t)$ and labor $l(t)$ as inputs. One could write the output $q(t)$ of this composite crop, as a function of water and labor, as follows:

$$q(t) = \{l_o(t) + l_m(t)\} \cdot \eta_q \cdot \frac{w(t)^{\psi}}{w(t)^{\psi} + \psi_0}. \tag{2}$$

In Equation (2), $l_o(t)$ and $l_m(t)$ are labor times dedicated to farming by the oldest and middle generations in the household, respectively, and η_q is the maximum output possible on one acre of land using one unit of labor and unlimited water. Parameters ψ_0 and ψ determine the shape of a non-linear relationship between water applied and output obtained. Specifically, ψ_0 can be defined as the level of water that leads to half of the maximum value of output η_q when the value of ψ is one and total labor time applied is also one. The above-specified agricultural production function assumes a sigmoid shape in water application, where output initially increases at an increasing rate, and once a certain level of water application is exceeded, it increases at a decreasing rate before finally plateauing.

The household's per-period profit function from farming $\pi(t)$ is defined as:

$$\pi(t) = p \cdot q(t) - k\{g(t), w(t)\}, \tag{3}$$

where p is the fixed price of the crop produced in year t, and $k\{g(t), w(t)\}$ is the cost of $w(t)$ units of groundwater applied. This cost is generally non-linear in groundwater depth $g(t)$ because decreasing levels of groundwater can make water abstraction costly. The stock of groundwater reservoir at time t grows with rainfall, net of any agricultural water abstraction, as follows:

$$\dot{g}(t) = -\omega(w(t)) + rain(t) \cdot \xi, \qquad (4)$$

where ξ is a parameter that converts rainfall into actual seepage and accumulation into the underground reservoir, and $\omega(w(t))$ is a non-linear function relating water abstraction to its impact on the stock of groundwater reservoir. Groundwater recharge is affected by the amount of irrigation water applied and evolves non-linearly depending upon several factors, such as soil porosity and underlying aquifer shape. I assume the representative household has exclusive access to this groundwater reservoir and the water level is not affected by drawdown from other nearby wells. In reality, groundwater reservoirs may be connected and are often used by multiple users, especially when there are ill-defined property rights. In such a situation, the concerned household will need to factor in the influences of exogenous as well as strategic behavior on groundwater levels when deciding their own long-term strategy.

The household maximizes the sum of per-period utilities $U(t)$ from consumption, as follows:

$$\int_0^\infty U[\varphi \cdot c(t), \{1 - \varphi - \tau_1(t) - \tau_2(t)\} \cdot g(t), \{\tau_1(t) + \tau_2(t)\} \cdot h(t)] \cdot \exp(-r \cdot t)dt, \quad (5)$$

where r is the discount rate. Later in the paper, I assume this utility to be of logarithmic form, which allows for risk aversion over consumption, and specifically assumes constant relative risk aversion (CRRA).

Each generation within the household has a total of one unit of time available to them annually. To simplify division of labor within the household, assume that the oldest generation only concerns itself with farming. The oldest generation's time constraint is therefore:

$$l_o(t) \leq 1. \qquad (6)$$

The middle generation is assumed to have the additional option of using $n(t)$ of their time to build social capital through networking, which is helpful in augmenting farm productivity. In reality, the oldest generation may also help build social capital, but we can ignore their contribution without any loss of generality. The middle generation's time constraint is therefore:

$$l_m(t) + n(t) \leq 1. \qquad (7)$$

The youngest generation can spend $edu(t)$ of their time acquiring skills, and use $l_y(t)$ of their time earning income based on their current skill level. The youngest generation's time constraint is thus:

$$l_y(t) + edu(t) \leq 1. \qquad (8)$$

The youngest generation concentrates on acquiring skills that are useful outside agriculture. The household invests in education of its youngest generation to acquire human capital $h(t)$, which leads to higher wages in the skilled sector. The maximum possible annual wage or income per unit of labor in the skilled sector is $\bar{i}$, which is assumed to be time invariant. However, as the youngest farmer's skill increases, their annual wage $i(t)$ gets closer to this maximum wage according to the following non-linear function:

$$i(t) = \bar{i} \cdot \frac{h(t)^{\alpha}}{h(t)^{\alpha} + \alpha_0} .$$ (9)

This functional form assumes that the marginal gain in wages initially increases and then decreases as the level of skill is raised. This assumption makes it increasingly difficult to achieve the maximum level of urban wage. Parameters α and α_0 (where $\alpha > 0$, $\alpha_0 > 0$) dictate the steepness of this function. As the skill level tends to infinity, $i(t)$ tends to $\bar{i}(t)$. This form also requires that a certain threshold level of skill must be acquired before the wage becomes significant.

Skill acquisition occurs through educational effort $edu(t)$ which comes at a financial cost of $c(edu(t))$ per unit of educational effort. In many economies, primary education is free; furthermore, the government provides additional incentives such as food through 'mid-day meal' schemes. The cost of acquiring skill in this model can be thought of as the additional cost above what is already freely available. The forgone agricultural labor of the youngest generation can also be considered as the additional (opportunity) cost of time spent acquiring skill.

If the youngest generation does not constantly augment their education, I assume their skill declines over time at a rate of δ_h. This mimics the formal education system, which requires continuous investment and progress through grades; otherwise, dropouts lose previously acquired skill. The skill-stock dynamic is given as:

$$\dot{h}(t) = \sigma \cdot edu(t) + \eta_h \cdot \frac{h(t)^{\nu}}{h(t)^{\nu} + v_0} - \delta_h \cdot h(t),$$ (10)

where σ converts the per-period educational time into human capital (or skill stock), with $edu(t) \leq 1$. In the above equation, I make an important assumption about the positive effect of one's own skill level $h(t)$ on the growth rate of future skills, as given by the feedback term $\eta_h \cdot \frac{h(t)^{\nu}}{h(t)^{\nu} + v_0}$. Parameters ν and v_0 determine the non-linear shape of the skill feedback function. This skill feedback term remains insignificant until a critical level of skill has been attained. As the level of skill increases (i.e., human capital accumulates), a critical threshold is reached at which time the trainee experiences a significant improvement in their overall skill growth level. In practical terms, this means that the trainee has reached an employable stage at which their skill level can automatically improve with time, even when no further formal educational effort is made.

The term η_h is the 'innate learning capability' of an individual, which is independent of educational effort. It leads to an automatic growth in skills once a critical mass of skill has been acquired. Below this critical mass, the individual's innate ability to grow skill is not significant as they are still in the formative stages of learning. In reality, this critical mass could vary amongst students, owing to such factors as genetic, environmental and motivational. Some achieve significant educational maturity early on, whereas for others it arrives later. Finally, in the absence of any further educational effort, net growth in skill stock will be influenced by the difference between the annual feedback growth and the annual depreciation rate in skill.

Next, I write out the dynamics associated with household financial wealth $m(t)$, which includes agricultural income, as well as non-agricultural income generated by the youngest generation:

$$\dot{m}(t) = p \cdot q(t) - k\{g(t), w(t)\} + \bar{i} \cdot \frac{h(t)^\alpha}{h(t)^\alpha + \alpha_0} \cdot l_y(t) - c(t) - c(edu(t)). \qquad (11)$$

I also introduce social capital and its influence on household agricultural earnings. I model the stock of accumulated social capital $s_k(t)$ as increasing in networking time $n(t)$, and evolving non-linearly in its own stock (of social capital), but declining in the absence of constant augmentation:

$$\dot{s}_k = f(n(t)) + \eta_s \cdot \frac{s_k(t)^{n_0}}{s_k(t)^{n_0} + n_1} - \delta_{s_k}(g(t)). \qquad (12)$$

In Equation (12), $f(n(t))$ is the non-linear effect of networking activity on social capital growth, with $f'(n(t)) > 0, f''(n(t)) < 0$. Networking activity can be thought of as social interaction processes in a farming community through which farmers receive and pass on information relevant to each other. In the current context, networking leads to accumulation of social capital, which augments farm productivity by providing crucial information about useful farming inputs and timing of their application, or by making available farm implements not owned by the farmer.

The term $\eta_s \cdot \frac{s_k(t)^{n_0}}{s_k(t)^{n_0} + n_1}$ provides feedback to the growth rate of social capital. Specifically, once a certain level of social capital is attained, that capital can continue to grow owing to previous investments in the social network. Social capital could also be augmented due to a growth in accumulated wealth. Higher financial wealth may allow the farmer to access bigger networks because they are in a better position to lend (or borrow) money.

An important assumption is made in the above equation that links social capital to natural resource capital. The rate of depreciation in social capital is determined by the parameter $\delta_{s_k}(g(t))$ – the decay rate of social capital – which is a function of groundwater level $g(t)$. The lower the groundwater level, the higher the rate of social capital decline. Reduced groundwater may cause conflicts between groundwater users, which will erode social capital through loss of networks that farmers rely upon to augment their productivity. Long-lasting declines in groundwater levels may force some farmers to migrate, thereby leading to additional loss of social capital. To put an upper bound on the groundwater-related rate of social capital decline, I assume that the relationship between groundwater level and rate of decline in social capital exhibits non-linearity, as in the following specification:

$$\delta_{s_k}(g(t)) = \delta_{0sk} \cdot (1 - \frac{g(t)^{\theta_0}}{g(t)^{\theta_0} + \theta_1}). \qquad (13)$$

We can now write the modified production function in agriculture as:

$$q(t) = \{l_o(t) + l_m(t)\} \cdot \{.75 + s_k(t)\} \cdot \eta_q \cdot \frac{w(t)^\psi}{w(t)^\psi + \psi_0}. \qquad (14)$$

The presence of social capital in the farm production function leads to higher output than what is possible in its absence, as long as the stock of social capital does not decline below 0.25 units. If the farmer has no social capital, the maximum possible output for any combination of inputs is lowered by 25% as compared to when the stock of social capital is 0.25 units. This decline of 25% could, in reality, be any number starting from zero. This kind of production function is more relevant in developing economies where means of production (such as technologies and instruments) are scarce and inefficient. Therefore, a farmer with good social capital can readily borrow resources (labor, energy, mechanical and physical) from others instead of having to own them personally. In the absence of such borrowed resources, their output would be lower.

Finally, we need to introduce dynamics pertaining to household preferences. This is accomplished by assigning further structure to the two weighting functions, as follows, such that they can change over time:

$$\tau_1(t) = 0.05 \cdot \frac{t^{25}}{t^{25} + 10^{24}} \tag{15}$$

$$\tau_2(t) = 0.05 \cdot \frac{\left(\frac{t}{2}\right)^{25}}{\left(\frac{t}{2}\right)^{25} + 10^{24}}. \tag{16}$$

$\tau_1(t)$ starts at a value of zero (at time zero) and reaches its maximum value of 0.05 after approximately 10 years (an arbitrarily chosen timeframe). $\tau_2(t)$ starts at a value of zero (at time zero) and reaches its maximum value of 0.05 after approximately 20 years. Therefore, if the initial weight placed on the consumption argument in the utility function was 0.9 and that on groundwater (agricultural lifestyle) was 0.1, then after 10 years, the weight on groundwater would reduce to 0.05 and that on human capital would increase to 0.05. After 20 years, the weight on groundwater would further reduce to zero whereas that on human capital would increase to 0.1. Figure 1 shows the shifting of weights placed on human capital in the utility function. After 10 years, the weights change from zero to 0.05;

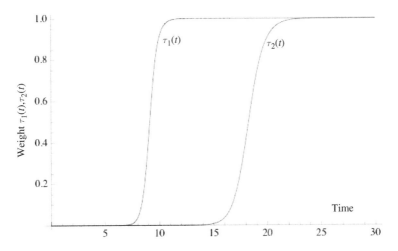

Figure 1. (Colour online) Time paths of weights placed on human capital in the utility function.

then, after another 10 years, they change to 0.1. The shift in weights could be made more gradual (less steep) through a tweaking of parameters in Equations (15) and (16).

The household's inter-temporal and inter-generational utility maximization problem can now be written as a current value Hamiltonian, $cvh(t)$, as follows:

$$cvh(t) = U[\phi \cdot c(t), \{1 - \phi - \tau_1(t) - \tau_2(t)\} \cdot g(t), \{\tau_1(t) + \tau_2(t)\} \cdot h(t)]$$

$$+ \mu_1(t) \cdot [-\omega(w(t)) + rain(t) \cdot \xi] + \mu_2(t) \cdot [\sigma \cdot edu(t) + \eta_h \cdot \frac{h(t)^v}{h(t)^v + v_0} - \delta \cdot h(t)]$$

$$+ \mu_3(t) \cdot \left[p \cdot q(t) - k\{g(t), w(t)\} + \bar{i} \cdot \frac{h(t)^\alpha}{h(t)^\alpha + \alpha_0} \cdot l_y(t) - c(t) - c(edu(t)) \right]$$

$$+ \mu_4(t) \cdot \left[f(n(t)) + \eta_s \cdot \frac{s_k(t)^{n_0}}{s_k(t)^{n_0} + n_1} - \delta_{s_k}(g(t)) \right]$$

$$+ L_0 \cdot (1 - l_o) + L_m \cdot \{1 - (l_m + n(t))\} + L_y \cdot \{1 - (l_y + edu(t))\}.$$

$$(17)$$

In the above equation, μ_1, μ_2, μ_3 and μ_4 are shadow prices of the groundwater stock, human capital stock, financial wealth and stock of social capital respectively. Variables L_0, L_m and L_y are Lagrangian constraints with respect to labor times spent by the oldest, middle and youngest generations, respectively.

Deriving the first-order condition with respect to water extraction, we can write:

$$\mu_1(t) \cdot \omega'(w(t)) = \mu_3 \cdot \pi'_{w(t)}(t).$$

$$(18)$$

The shadow price of groundwater is directly related to the shadow price of financial wealth. The first-order condition with respect to human capital (i.e., educational effort) is written as:

$$\mu_2(t) \cdot \sigma - L_y = \mu_3 \cdot c'(edu(t)).$$

$$(19)$$

Using the above derivations, we can now write:

$$\mu_1(t) = \frac{\pi'_{w(t)}(t)}{\omega'(w(t)) \cdot c'(edu(t))} \cdot \{\mu_2(t) \cdot \sigma - L_y\}.$$

$$(20)$$

Equation (20) requires that, along an optimal resource allocation path, the shadow price of groundwater must equal the adjusted shadow price of human capital, where the adjustment factor is a ratio of the marginal profitability of water in agriculture to the marginal cost of educational effort.

Finally, we introduce the risk of irreversible groundwater loss, which is assumed to be governed by an exponential distribution (Clarke & Reed, 1994; Tsur & Zemel, 1994, 2004). The hazard rate of groundwater loss is given by $\lambda(t)$, where the probability that the event will occur after time t is given as $\exp(-\lambda(t))$. The change in the accumulated hazard is defined as:

$$\dot{\lambda}(t) = haz_0 \cdot \exp\{-g(t) \cdot haz_1\}.$$

$$(21)$$

Rewriting the current value Hamilton to include the risk of irreversible groundwater loss and payoffs in pre and post-groundwater-loss scenarios, we get:

$$cvh(t) = U[\varphi \cdot c(t), \{1 - \varphi - \tau_1(t) - \tau_2(t)\} \cdot g(t), \{\tau_1(t) + \tau_2(t)\} \cdot h(t)] \cdot \exp(-\lambda(t))$$
$$+ V_{post}[m(t), h(t)] \cdot \dot{\lambda}(t) \cdot \exp(-\lambda(t)) + \mu_1(t) \cdot [-\omega(w(t)) + rain(t) \cdot \xi]$$
$$+ \mu_2(t) \cdot [\sigma \cdot edu(t) + \eta_h \cdot \frac{h(t)^v}{h(t)^v + v_0} - \delta \cdot h(t)]$$
$$+ \mu_3(t) \cdot \left[p \cdot q(t) - k\{g(t), w(t)\} + \bar{i} \cdot \frac{h(t)^\alpha}{h(t)^\alpha + \alpha_0} \cdot l_y(t) - c(t) - c(edu(t)) \right]$$
$$+ \mu_4(t) \cdot \left[f(n(t)) + \eta_s \cdot \frac{s_k(t)^{n_0}}{s_k(t)^{n_0} + n_1} - \delta_{s_k}(g(t)) \right]$$
$$+ \mu_5(t) \cdot [haz_0 \cdot \exp(-g(t) \cdot haz_1)] + L_0 \cdot (1 - l_o) + L_m \cdot \{1 - (l_m + n(t))\}$$
$$+ L_y \cdot \{1 - (l_y + edu(t))\}$$

$$(22)$$

where $V_{post}[m(t), h(t)]$ is the post-groundwater-loss value function. This value function depends on the level of financial wealth and human capital at the time of groundwater loss. In the post-loss scenario, only the youngest generation is assumed to be working (in formal or informal sectors outside of agriculture), whereas the oldest and middle generations are assumed to be unemployed. Further, I assume that the post-loss utility function does not include either groundwater or human capital stocks. When the household loses groundwater, farming ceases to be a livelihood option and it must rely on acquired human capital to ensure sustenance in the post-loss world. Therefore, whereas the pre-loss utility function adds weight to human capital in the utility function to indicate the household's transitional aspirations, the post-loss world excludes it to reflect the shift in preferences entirely on consumption to ensure survival.

Introducing the risk of groundwater loss may cause the household to be more conservative in its effort to accumulate human capital. This is because education is expensive, requiring crop-derived income to cover its cost, which in turn requires consumption of groundwater resources. If the resulting decline in groundwater is too rapid, it will threaten the long-term sustainability of the groundwater reservoir, and hence the household's future ability to grow crops and generate funds to invest in education. This unsustainable depletion of groundwater may even jeopardize the household's occupational transition plan. To explore this idea and generate more concrete insights, we now turn to a numerical simulation of the above problem.

3. A numerical example

Parameters for the base-case simulation are presented in Table 1. We also assume no risk of groundwater loss, a weight of 0.9 on consumption (that is $\phi = 0.9$), and a weight of 0.1 on the groundwater reservoir level in the household's utility function. We re-define the utility function accordingly:

$$U(t) = [0.9 \cdot \log(c(t)) + (\tau_1(t) + \tau_2(t)) \cdot \log(h(t)) + (0.1 - \tau_1(t) - \tau_2(t))$$
$$\cdot \log(g(t)/60)]$$

$$(23)$$

Deviating from the theoretical model, the time horizon of the family is assumed to be 50 years. With a discount rate of 5%, a unit of utility derived at the end of 50 years would

Table 1. Base-case parameter values.

Parameters	Values (units)	Description
r	0.05 (scalar)	Discount rate
ψ	3 (scalar)	Non-linear parameter in water yield relationship
ψ_0	20 (scalar)	Non-linear parameter in water yield relationship
λ_0	0 (scalar)	Initial level of cumulative hazard
η_q	0.75 (tonnes)	Maximum crop output possible without social capital
ξ	0.002 (scalar)	Factor for converting rainwater into groundwater recharge
$mean$	400 mm	Mean of annual rainfall
std	1 mm	Standard deviation of annual rainfall
p	40 (rupees per kilo)	Price of crop
g_0	120 (index)	Initial level of groundwater
m_0	5 (thousand rupees)	Initial level of financial wealth
ϕ	0.9	Weight on consumption in the utility function
$1 - \phi$	0.1	Starting weight on groundwater stock in the utility function
σ	0.15	Effect of educational effort on human capital accumulation
η_h	0.3	Innate capability to learn
δ_h	0.05	Rate of depreciation in human capital
η_s	0.01 (scalar)	Maximum feedback growth in social capital per period
v	7 (scalar)	Non-linear parameters determining the shape of the skill feedback term
v_0	100 (scalar)	Non-linear parameters determining the shape of the skill feedback term
α	2 (scalar)	Non-linear parameters determining the shape of the wage-skill relationship
α_0	1 (scalar)	Non-linear parameters determining the shape of the wage-skill relationship
δ_{0sk}	0.04 (scalar)	Maximum possible decay in social capital per period
θ_0, θ_1	3 (scalar), 100000 (scalar)	Non-linear parameters determining social capital decay rate
n_0, n_1	3 (scalar), 1 (scalar)	Non-linear parameters for feedback effect of social capital
$c(edu(t))$	$100 \cdot edu(t)$ (thousand rupees)	Cost of educational effort in terms of thousands of rupees per unit of time
haz_0	0.05	Exogenous component of the hazard rate for irreversible groundwater loss
haz_1	0.01	Parameter adjusting the effect of groundwater on hazard rate of its loss
$\bar{i}$	600 (thousand rupees)	Maximum skilled wages per unit of labor
g_0	120 (scalar)	Initial level of groundwater reservoir

have a present value of only 0.09 units. Increasing the time horizon to 100 or 200 years may capture an infinite horizon problem more precisely, but it does not change the groundwater extraction time path and changes the overall utility by only a few units. Furthermore, as we see later, groundwater does not last more than 25–30 years under the household's optimal extraction plan. The base-case groundwater level is assumed to start at 120 units. The stock of human capital stock, which starts at zero units, can reach up to two or three units.

Initially, the oldest generation farmer places weight only on consumption (0.9) and groundwater (0.1), thereby ignoring human capital. However, after 10 years, when the middle generation farmer's preferences become dominant within the household, weights on groundwater and human capital in the utility function are each changed to 0.05, with consumption continuing to receive the remaining 0.9 weight. Finally, after another

10 years, the weight on groundwater is reduced to zero, while that on human capital is increased to 0.1, to represent the youngest generation. The weight on consumption (0.9) never changes its value throughout the entire time horizon.

Groundwater dynamics are modelled as follows:

$$\dot{g}(t) = -w(t) + rain(t) \cdot 0.002. \tag{24}$$

I intentionally keep the groundwater hydrology linear, which is simplistic, but avoids having to tease apart the non-linear impact of groundwater depletion on simulation results from the impacts of other non-linear phenomenon, such as social capital or skill dynamics.

The social capital accumulation function is assigned further structure to relate the non-linear effect of networking on social capital accumulation, as follows:

$$\dot{s}_k(t) = 0.05 \cdot \log\{0.1 + 3 \cdot n(t)\} + \eta_s \cdot \frac{s_k(t)^{n_0}}{s_k(t)^{n_0} + n_1} - \delta_{s_k}(g(t)). \tag{25}$$

The marginal effects of networking decline with effort as represented through the log function in Equation (25).

The post-loss value function, which captures the sum of utilities derived in time periods following an irreversible groundwater loss, is as follows:

$$v_{post}[m(t), h(t)] = [63.54 + 0.05014 \cdot m(t) + 46.72 \cdot h(t) - 0.00004116 \cdot m(t)^2 \\ - 0.01627 \cdot h(t) \cdot m(t) - 8.998 \cdot h(t)^2]. \tag{26}$$

This function was calibrated by optimizing the post-loss problem for several starting levels of wealth and skill. Calibration was done in MATLAB using the surface fitting option. In contrast, the optimal utility functions for each starting combination of human capital and financial wealth were solved for in GAMS using the non-linear solver. The post-loss value function changes and is recalibrated, as follows, when a lower educational effectiveness is assumed (by reducing the value of σ from its base-case value of 0.15 to 0.1):

$$v_{post}[m(t), h(t)] = [46.96 + 0.05456 \cdot m(t) + 61.86 \cdot h(t) - 0.00004087 \cdot m(t)^2 \\ - 0.01864 \cdot h(t) \cdot m(t) - 12.19 \cdot h(t)^2]. \tag{27}$$

Finally, when the maximum skilled wage is halved from its base-case level of 600 thousand rupees, we get the following new post-loss value function:

$$v_{post}[m(t), h(t)] = [33.46 + 0.09632 \cdot m(t) + 61.12 \cdot h(t) - 0.00009453 \cdot m(t)^2 \\ - 0.02972 \cdot h(t) \cdot m(t) - 11.88 \cdot h(t)^2]. \tag{28}$$

As a side-note, the post-loss value functions in Equations (26) through (28) could have been calibrated, instead, using non-linear least squares (after obtaining data points through repeated optimization of various starting-state levels). For instance, I verified for equation (28) that the non-linear least squares method in STATA leads to coefficient estimates very similar to those obtained through the CFTOOL option in MATLAB. They both lead to similar levels of R^2 (0.95).

Figure 2 depicts groundwater outcomes for various scenarios performed under this numerical exercise. The highest long-term groundwater levels are obtained when the oldest generation assigns a relatively high weight (0.1) to the groundwater argument in the utility function. Groundwater preservation also increases when the maximum urban wage ($\bar{i}$) is halved from its base-case level of 600 thousand. This is clearly because the benefit of accumulating human capital (at the cost of depleting natural capital) has declined. When this 'halving of the urban wage' scenario is paired with a risk of irreversible groundwater loss, groundwater levels are depleted to much lower levels than in the absence of such risk. This is due primarily to the discounting effect brought in through risk. A lower educational effectiveness has a similar effect as that of a lower $\bar{i}$ in the urban sector; that is, it promotes groundwater conservation. Note that, in relevant figures, $\bar{i}$ is referred to as 'ibar'.

Other scenarios that lead to a lower groundwater level, compared to the base case, include the following: an irreversible groundwater loss risk with an $\bar{i}$ of 600 thousand; a reduction in the social capital cost of groundwater depletion (i.e., $\delta_{s_k}\{g(t)\} = 0.01$); and groundwater and human capital being given no weight in the utility function.

Figure 3 depicts the corresponding social capital outcomes for the above scenarios. Notice that, in the presence of a lower urban wage or lower effectiveness of education, the family invests heavily in social capital accumulation, to boost agricultural productivity. It

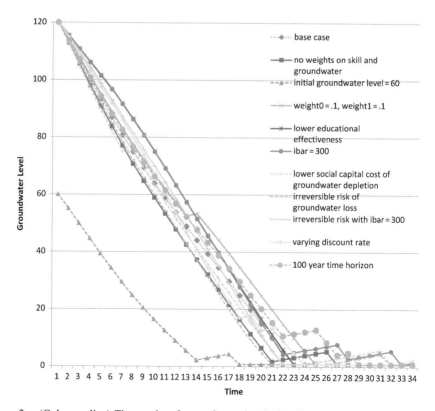

Figure 2.   (Colour online) Time paths of groundwater levels for all scenarios.

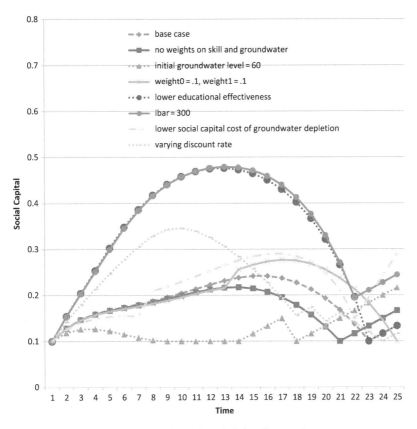

Figure 3.   (Colour online) Time paths of social capital for all scenarios.

would be interesting to test, empirically, whether higher social capital in some cases may reflect a household's efforts to offset relatively low productivity of other forms of capital (such as human capital). The lowest social capital investment occurs when starting groundwater endowments are much lower at 60 units. In this case, the household uses a rapid transition approach to acquire human capital, as described later in more detail.

Earlier in the paper, I described an assumption that as groundwater level declines, tensions among users rise, and social networks begin to break down. Conversely, a high groundwater level automatically reduces the depreciation rate of social capital, hence augmenting the stock of social capital in the long term. It is logical, then, that scenarios in which a higher weight is placed on groundwater in the utility function result not only in higher groundwater levels, but also higher social capital stock. If we relax the assumed relationship between groundwater level and social capital, such that the social capital depreciation effects of groundwater depletion are smaller, then groundwater is depleted faster, as noted earlier in Figure 2. In this case, however, even though groundwater is depleted faster, social capital actually increases. This has to do with a larger networking effect (see Figure 4), as discussed next.

The networking effect, along with the groundwater level, determines the eventual stock of social capital. Thus, in the scenario where the starting groundwater level is halved compared to the base case, the resulting higher depreciation rate of social capital can be offset with a higher networking effort. By optimally mixing higher networking effort

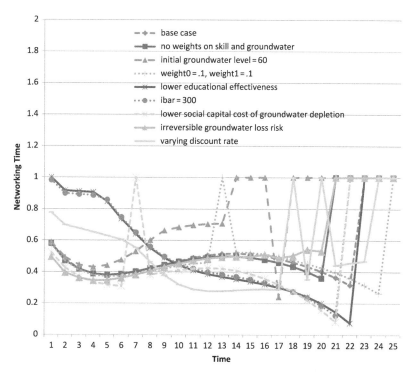

Figure 4. (Colour online) Networking efforts over time for various scenarios.

(i.e., social capital) with educational effort (i.e., human capital), it may be possible to transition the youngest generation into high-skilled urban labor, even under relatively low water-endowment situations.

Before we look at skill outcomes, however, let us revisit Figure 4, which shows optimal networking effort for various scenarios. An interesting switch in networking effort occurs through time under scenarios in which urban wage or education effectiveness is lower. Under these scenarios, in the first 10 years, a larger weight on groundwater in the utility function combined with a lower urban wage results in greater emphasis on agricultural productivity through increased networking by the middle generation. However, after the first 10 years, when the weight on human capital becomes comparable to that on ground-water, the middle generation's networking efforts decline significantly. Instead, they begin investing more in efforts to augment the youngest generation's skill (human capital). This switch is depicted in the time paths of skill outcomes, which are discussed next.

Skill or human capital accumulation time paths are depicted in Figure 5. Predictably, the lowest skill levels are obtained when the urban wage or educational effectiveness is low. Skill investment is zero for the first 10 years, but starts to pick up as the weight on human capital increases through time. The highest skill levels are achieved when a risk of irreversible groundwater loss is introduced. Skill outcomes for other scenarios hover closely around those for the base case.

Household consumption outcomes are depicted in Figure 6. Although the risk of an irreversible loss of groundwater leads to rapid skill accumulation, it also leads to lower long-term consumption. This is due, in part, to higher consumption sacrifices required to accumulate skill. Furthermore, a risk of irreversible groundwater loss induces the farmer

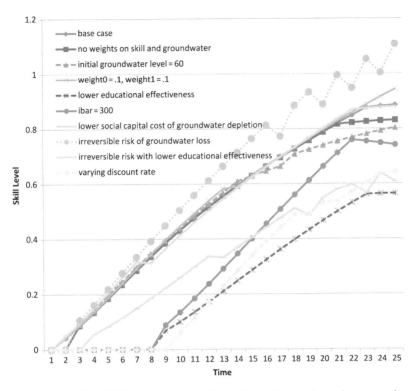

Figure 5. (Colour online) Skill-level outcomes depicted over time under various scenarios.

to amass wealth while water is still available to pay for future consumption and skill investment. This leads to lower relative consumption compared to other scenarios. Similarly, lower groundwater endowments (as opposed to a risk of groundwater loss) combined with lower urban wages or lower educational effectiveness also lead to lower consumption outcomes.

Finally, we consider the possibility that time discounting across generations may differ. Assume the oldest generation is more patient, but the middle and youngest generations are twice as impatient. That is, the discount rate chosen by the oldest generation is 0.05, but after 10 years, it rises to 0.1 and stays at that level until the end of the time horizon. The equation marking a shift in the discount rate is formulated as:

$$r(t) = 0.05 + 0.05 \cdot \frac{t^{25}}{t^{25} + 10^{24}}. \tag{29}$$

As shown in the previous set of figures, higher future discounting by the middle and youngest generations leads to a lower level of skill accumulation, and higher consumption in the early years at the cost of lower consumption in the future years. However, the groundwater outcome is much higher for the first 10 years, compared to the base case, but declines later on. The household needs to ensure a higher groundwater outcome because there is no skill-based income in the future due to discount-induced under-investment in skills and social capital. This interesting outcome implies that inter-generational differences in discounting may work against a smooth exit out of agriculture.

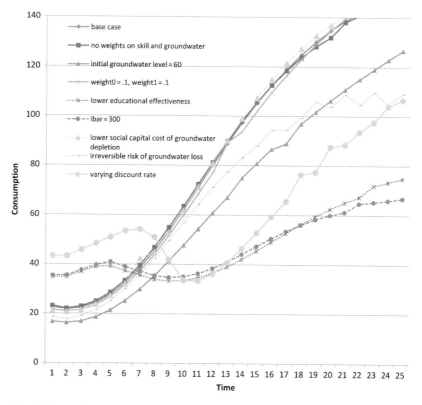

Figure 6. (Colour online) Time paths of annual consumption for all scenarios.

4. Summary and concluding remarks

Increasing instances of drought are making farming-based livelihoods unsustainable for many households around the world. Reduced productivity and surmounting debts force some to exit farming abruptly. For families who have persisted, farming might nonetheless not be the youngest generations' preferred long-term occupational choice, due in part to pessimistic forecasts of future water availability. For such households, exit from agriculture is a more gradual process of occupational transitioning that involves multiple generations.

The complexities of inter-generational decision making in farming households, where values and preferences may differ across generations, are accentuated when climate change causes a long-term risk of irreversible groundwater loss. When the natural resource base is threatened by climate change, and there is a pressing need to enhance short-term agricultural productivity to facilitate accumulation of human capital, all three generations within the household are hard-pressed to ensure a smooth transition. One complication is that different generations within the household may hold different preferences over the various capital stocks they own or desire. Difficult tradeoffs between these capital assets may be necessary for a successful occupational transition to occur.

I have modelled the possibility that preferences change across generations using a dynamic utility function, where the weights placed on various types of capital change over time as one generation gets older and the next generation's preferences become dominant. The oldest generation places a higher weight on preserving groundwater because this also preserves their agricultural way of life. The middle generation must seek a balance between the needs of the oldest and youngest generations. The youngest generation invests only in human capital accumulation because a future in agriculture is seen as increasingly unviable.

Several insights are derived from the theoretical model and numerical example. Utility functions that explicitly incorporate groundwater as an argument, via the oldest generation's preferences for an agricultural lifestyle, lead to better groundwater outcomes than utility functions that do not. This is evident by comparing groundwater outcomes in scenarios where groundwater and human capital are included in the utility function to the scenario where human capital and groundwater are excluded from the utility function. In the latter case, not only is the groundwater level lower, the human capital obtained is also relatively lower. However, the risk of irreversible groundwater loss accelerates human capital accumulation as a means to achieve a smooth transition out of agriculture. Unfortunately, this necessitates more rapid groundwater depletion.

Communities with lower water endowments, as opposed to risk of irreversible groundwater loss, might also use this same strategy to ensure a smooth transition out of agriculture. The middle generation plays a key role by investing early-on in networking to accumulate social capital, which leads to higher productivity in agriculture. Proceeds from agriculture are then invested to augment the youngest generation's human capital. The middle generation's accumulation of social capital also leads to feedback growths in this stock, thereby reducing the need for further networking in later years and allowing for extra labor allocation to agriculture. By optimally mixing groundwater extraction, networking, and educational investments, the farming family can accumulate the desirable quantities of natural, social, and human capital to ensure a successful transition out of an agriculture sector that is becoming less viable.

Differences across farming generations can make a smooth exit out of agriculture challenging though. One such difference is the degree of time discounting. A situation in which younger generations are more impatient than the oldest generation could lead to outcomes that are conducive to neither natural resource preservation nor human capital accumulation. Another potential difference among generations is the relative values they place on an agricultural versus urban lifestyle. I assume that the oldest generation values an agricultural lifestyle more, whereas the youngest generation values a non-agricultural lifestyle; the middle generation simply assists in this transition. While not considered in the paper, it is possible that a highly skewed preference for groundwater or social capital could lead to significant under-investment in human capital and failure to transition out of farming for the youngest generations.

In agricultural sectors, especially in developing economies, social capital might also directly enter the household's utility function. Besides augmenting farm productivity, social capital could serve the purpose of building self-identity. A farmer with higher social capital may have a higher sense of self-worth, in the absence of more modern indicators, such as monetary wealth. Farmers might also accumulate social capital as a benevolent activity to help build and sustain community identity. If social capital is a component of a household's utility function, there could be additional challenges to inter-generational transitioning because investment in social capital is likely to have an opportunity cost.

From the outside looking in, farming families that appear to be persevering in agriculture may actually be planning fundamental changes, driven by how long they intend to stay in agriculture. A household's plan for transitioning out of agriculture is affected by each generation's unique lifestyle preferences and time discounting. In turn, their transition plan has direct implications for depletion or accumulation of natural, social and human capital stocks. Farmers, especially in the developing world, rely on various combinations of capital to sustain their livelihoods. Climate-change-induced water scarcity can have significant bearing on how such capital types are managed and traded off. These choices not only affect the household's long-term welfare outcome, but could also affect the demographic composition and sustainability of agriculture in the long-term.

Policies aimed at making agriculture more sustainable, either economically or environmentally, should be sensitive to inter-generational decision making, including nuances in preferences across generations, and complex interactions and tradeoffs among natural, social and human capital stocks. In particular, policies aimed at augmenting groundwater may turn out to be less effective in absence of complementary support programs that subsidize farmers' human capital accumulation cost, as, when left to their own means, farmers may overdraw groundwater to pay for human capital accumulation. Finally, provision of better farm technology that makes farming more productive can also reduce investments in social capital, which is targeted at augmenting crop output, thereby freeing up resources for other productive ventures by farmers. This is especially true when social capital is adversely impacted by a reduction in the natural capital base of a region.

Acknowledgements

This paper was completed while the author was a visiting scholar at the Yale School of Forestry and Environmental Studies. The author would like to thank the hosts for their generous hospitality. The author would like to thank two anonymous reviewers for their helpful comments and the Associate Editor, Dannele Peck for providing valuable suggestions and extensive editing of the paper.

References

Antoci, A. (2009). Environmental degradation as engine of undesirable economic growth via self-protection consumption choices. *Ecological Economics, 68*, 1385–1397. doi:10.1016/j.ecolecon.2008.09.009

Azariadis, C. (1993). *Inter-temporal macro-economics*. Oxford: Basil Blackwell Scientific Publications.

Becker, G., & Tomes, N. (1979). An equilibrium theory of the distribution of income and inter-generational mobility. *Journal of Political Economy, 87*(6), 1153–1189. doi:10.1086/260831

Bisin, A., & Verdier, T. (2001). The economics of cultural transmission and the dynamics of preferences. *Journal of Economic Theory, 97*, 298–319. doi:10.1006/jeth.2000.2678

Carey, J. M., & Zilberman, D. (2002). A model of investment under uncertainty: Modern irrigation technology and emerging markets in water. *American Journal of Agricultural Economics, 84*(1), 171–183. doi:10.1111/1467-8276.00251

Clarke, H R., & Reed, W. J. (1994). Consumption/pollution tradeoffs in an environment vulnerable to pollution related catastrophic collapse. *Journal of Economic Dynamics and Control, 18*, 991–1010. doi:10.1016/0165-1889(94)90042-6

Department of Agriculture, Fisheries and Forestry. (2012). *Drought in Australia: Context, policy and management*. Retrieved from http://www.daff.gov.au/_media/documents/abares/publications/client_reports/drought-in-australia-2012.pdf

Emran, M. S., & Shilpi, F. (2011). Intergenerational occupational mobility in rural economy: Evidence from Nepal and Vietnam. *Journal of Human Resources, 46*(2), 427–458. doi:10.1353/jhr.2011.0009

Emran, M. S., & Sun, Y. (2011). Magical transition? Intergenerational educational and occupational mobility in rural China: 1988–2002. Retrieved from http://www.econ.yale.edu/conference/neudc11/papers/paper_055.pdf

Fafchamps, M., & Minten, B. (2002). Returns to social network capital among traders. *Oxford Economic Papers, 54*(2), 173–206. doi:10.1093/oep/54.2.173

Finkelstein, A., Luttmer, E. F. P., & Notowidigdo, M. J. (2013). What good is wealth without health? The effect of health on the marginal utility of consumption. *Journal of the European Economic Association, 11*(s1), 221–258. doi:10.1111/j.1542-4774.2012.01101.x

Government of India. (2012). MGNREGA Sameeksha: An anthology of research studies on the Mahatma Gandhi National Rural Employment Guarantee Act, 2005, New Delhi: Government of India, Ministry of Rural Development.

Hanigan, I. C., Butler, C. D., Kokic, P. N., & Hutchinson, M. F. (2012). Suicide and drought in New South Wales, Australia, 1970–2007. *Proceedings of the National Academy of Sciences of the United States of America, 109*(35), 13950–13955. doi:10.1073/pnas.1112965109

Hartman, D., & Arata, A. (2011). *Measuring social capital and innovation in poor agricultural communities: The case of Chaparra, Peru.* FZID Discussion Paper, No. 30–2011. Retrieved from http://opus.uni-hohenheim.de/volltexte/2011/622/pdf/fzid_dp_2011_30_Pyka2.pdf

Harvey, C. A., Rakotobe, Z. L., Rao, N. S., Dave, R., Razafimahatratra, H., Rabarijohn, R. H., … MacKinnon, J. L. (2014). Extreme vulnerability of smallholder farmers to agricultural risk and climate change in Madagascar. *Philosophical Transactions of the Royal Society B, 369*(1639), 20130089.

Hazell, P. B., & Hess, U. (2010). Drought insurance for agricultural development and food security in dryland areas. *Food Security, 2*(4), 395–405. doi:10.1007/s12571-010-0087-y

Huffman, W. E. (2001). Chapter 7 Human capital: Education and agriculture. *Handbook of Agricultural Economics, 1*(A), 333–381. doi:10.1016/S1574-0072(01)10010-1

Kerr, J., Pangare, G., & Panagre, V. L. (2002). *Watershed development projects in India: An evaluation.* Research Report 127, International Food Policy Research Institute. Retrieved from http://www.ifpri.org/sites/default/files/pubs/pubs/abstract/127/rr127.pdf

Khanna, M., Epohue, O. F., & Hornbaker, R. (1999). Site-specific crop management: Adoption pattern and trends. *Review of Agricultural Economics, 21*(Fall/Winter), 455–472.

Krishna, A., & Uphoff, N. (1999). *Mapping and measuring social capital: A conceptual and empirical study of collective action for conserving and developing watersheds in Rajasthan, India.* Social Capital Initiative Working Paper No. 13. Washington D.C.: World Bank. Retrieved from http://siteresources.worldbank.org/INTSOCIALCAPITAL/Resources/Social-Capital-Initiative-Working-Paper-Series/SCI-WPS-13.pdf

Löffler, A. (2001). A μ–σ risk aversion paradox and wealth dependent utility. *Journal of Risk and Uncertainty, 23*(1), 57–73. doi:10.1023/A:1011164615592

Morton, J. F. (2007). The impact of climate change on smallholder subsistence agriculture. *Proceedings of the National Academy of Sciences of the United States of America, 104*(50), 19680–19685. doi:10.1073/pnas.0701855104

Nagaraj, K. (2008). *Farmers' suicides in India: Magnitudes, trends and spatial patterns.* Madras Institute of Development Studies. Retrieved from http://www.macroscan.org/anl/mar08/pdf/farmers_suicides.pdf

Peck, D. E., & Adams, R. M. (2012). Farm-level impacts of climate change: Alternative approaches for modeling uncertainty. In A. Dinar & R. Mendelsohn (Eds.), *Handbook on climate change and agriculture.* Cheltenham, Gloucestershire: Edward Elgar Publishing.

Putnam, R. D. (1993). *Making democracy work. Civic traditions in modern Italy.* Princeton, NJ: Princeton University Press.

Putnam, R. D. (1995). Bowling alone: America's declining social capital. *Journal of Democracy, 6*(1), 65–78. doi:10.1353/jod.1995.0002

Putnam, R. D. (2014). *Social capital: Measurement and consequences.* OECD report. Retrieved from http://www.oecd.org/innovation/research/1825848.pdf

Ranjan, R. (2013). Mathematical modeling of drought resilience in agriculture. *Natural Resource Modeling, 26*(2), 237–258. doi:10.1111/j.1939-7445.2012.00136.x

Ranjan, R., & Athalye, S. (2009). Drought resilience in agriculture: The role of technological options, land use dynamics and risk perception. *Natural Resource Modeling, 22*(3), 437–462. doi:10.1111/j.1939-7445.2009.00044.x

Rodell, M., Velicogna, I., & Famiglietti, J. S. (2009). Satellite based estimates of groundwater depletion in India. *Nature, 460*, 999–1002. doi:10.1038/nature08238

Roncoli, C., Ingram, K., & Kirshen, P. (2001). The costs and risks of coping with drought: livelihood impacts and farmers' responses in Burkina Faso. *Climate Research, 19*, 119–132. doi:10.3354/cr019119

Schuck, E. C., Frasier, W. M., Webb, R. S., Ellingson, LJ., & Umberger, W. J. (2005). Adoption of more technically efficient irrigation systems as a drought response. *International Journal of Water Resources Development*, 21(4), 651–662. doi:10.1080/07900620500363321

Taylor, J E., & Martin, P. L. (2001). Chapter 9 Human capital: Migration and rural population change. *Handbook of Agricultural Economics*, 1(A), 457–511. doi:10.1016/S1574-0072(01)10012-5

Taylor, R. G., Scanlon, B., Döll, P., Rodell, M., Beek, R., Wada, Y., … Treidel, H. (2012). Groundwater and climate change. *Nature Climate Change*, 3, 322–329. doi:10.1038/nclimate1744

Trenberth, K. E., Dai, A., van der Schrier, G., Jones, P. D., Barichivich, J., Briffa, K. R., & Sheffield, J. (2014). Global warming and changes in drought. *Nature Climate Change*, 4(17), 17–22. doi:10.1038/nclimate2067

Tsur, Y., & Zemel, A. (1994). Endangered species and natural resource exploitation: Extinction versus coexistence. *Natural Resource Modeling*, 8(4), 389–413.

Tsur, Y., & Zemel, A. (2004). Endangered aquifers: Groundwater management under threats of catastrophic events. *Water Resources Research*, 40(6), W06S20. doi:10.1029/2003WR002168

Vermeulen, F. (2002). Collective household models: Principles and main results. *Journal of Economic Surveys*, 16(4), 533–564. doi:10.1111/1467-6419.00177

Ye, T., Shi, P., Wang, J., Liu, L., Fan, Y., & Hu, J. (2012). China's drought disaster risk management: Perspective of severe droughts in 2009–2010. *International Journal of Disaster Risk Science*, 3(2), 84–97. doi:10.1007/s13753-012-0009-z

Zilberman, D., Dinar, A., McDougall, N., Khanna, M., Brown, C., & Castillo, F. (1995). *Individual and institutional responses to drought: The case of California agriculture*. Working Paper, Department of Agricultural and Resource Economics, University of California, Berkeley, CA.

Can social resilience inform SA/SIA for adaptive planning for climate change in vulnerable regions?

Allan Dale[a], Karen J. Vella[b] and Alison Cottrell[c]

[a]Cairns Institute, James Cook University, Cairns, QLD, Australia; [b]Griffith School of Environment, Griffith University, Gold Coast, QLD, Australia; [c]Centre for Disaster Studies, School of Earth & Environmental Sciences, James Cook University, Cairns, QLD, Australia

Social resilience concepts are gaining momentum in environmental planning through an emerging understanding of the socio-ecological nature of biophysical systems. There is a disconnect, however, between these concepts and the sociological and psychological literature related to social resilience. Further still, both schools of thought are not well connected to the concepts of social assessment (SA) and social impact assessment (SIA) that are the more standard tools supporting planning and decision-making. This raises questions as to how emerging social resilience concepts can translate into improved SA/SIA practices to inform regional-scale adaptation. Through a review of the literature, this paper suggests that more cross-disciplinary integration is needed if social resilience concepts are to have a genuine impact in helping vulnerable regions tackle climate change.

1. Introduction

Many regions across the globe are highly vulnerable to climate change and associated water-related disasters (Hare, Cramer, Schaeffer, Battaglini, & Jaeger, 2011). Most vulnerable regions, however, are not unique in that consequent policy and planning interventions need to focus on supporting regional-scale social adaptation in order to avoid or to mitigate key community and natural resource impacts (Gooch & Rigano, 2010). Past approaches to planning in regions (including climate adaptation) across the globe have tended to predominantly focus on interventions dominated by biophysical and engineering knowledge (Dale, Taylor, & Lane, 2001; Stanley, 2010). Community adaptation in the face of climate change, however, needs to respond to many emerging social and economic factors such as:

- Demographic change within communities, including new arrivals with limited experience of extreme events;
- Vulnerabilities due to low income, high unemployment and under-employment, boom-bust cycles and related issues of housing access and affordability;
- Strained emergency response systems, particularly outside major urban areas, including infrastructure (roads, hospitals and shelters) vulnerable to major events;
- Specific vulnerabilities of core economic industries (e.g., tourism and agriculture); and

- A high proportion of significant physical and mental health impacts compounded by well-defined health, justice and social disparities (Dale et al., 2011).

As a highly complex social and ecological dilemma, climate change challenges traditional approaches to policy, institutions and management. The multi-dimensionality of climate change problems, the spatial and temporal disparities between cause and effect, and the divergent impact of different governance arrangements on social and ecological behavior in complex systems make it difficult to find effective policy responses. Scale-based responses need to overcome dynamic and discontinuous behavior and achieve desired outcomes in natural and human systems (Holling, 1973).

The realization that ecological systems are complex and dynamic led to exploration of the ability of ecosystems to absorb perturbations (Adger, 2000). Consequently, resilience thinking emerged in the ecological literature from the mid-1970s, enabling consideration of thresholds or triggers that drive ecosystems into new steady states (Folke, 2006). Because of its applicability in conceptualizing change in complex ecosystems, many ecologists (with a typically strong focus on cause and effect relationships) and collaborating sociologists began to consider the application of ecological resilience concept to complex socio-political systems (Adger, 2000; Berkes, Colding, & Folke, 2003). This led to the emergence of the concept of socio-ecological systems in the biological literature.

Several authors, however, have identified challenges in meshing both ecological and social resilience concepts, and at least two problems have been identified within the literature:

(1) Resilience concepts had already co-evolved in isolation in the social sciences literature, though with significant conceptual difference (Béné, Newsham, Davies, Ulrichs, & Godfrey-Wood, 2014; Berkes & Ross, 2013; Maclean, Cuthill, & Ross, 2013); and

(2) Linked human societies act differently to ecosystems, so ecological concepts, while useful, are not fully inter-changeable with social ones (Brown & Westaway, 2011; Dale et al., 2011; Kulig, Edge, Townshend, Lightfoot, & Reimer, 2013; Ross, Cuthill, Maclean, Jansen, & Witt, 2010).

In literature about resilience concepts and community adaptation, it has tended to be the ecologists who have driven the debate in their attempts to seamlessly migrate resilience concepts into what has been a traditionally social science domain (Walker, Hollin, Carpenter, & Kinzig, 2004). In doing so, however, we would agree with Berkes and Ross (2013) and Béné et al. (2014) that there has been some disconnect between the concepts of social resilience that have emerged within the ecological and sociological/psychological sciences literature. Adger (2000), for example, concludes that while there is a link between ecological and social resilience concepts, this may primarily relate to the dependence of different social groups on particular natural resources, and that it is not clear that resilient ecosystems might enable resilient communities, or vice versa.

We further contend that this disconnect exacerbates problems emerging from the fact that there have been few effective linkages drawn between social resilience concepts and the social assessment (SA) and social impact assessment (SIA) literature, these being commonly used and practical analytical tools for supporting community change and the sociological tools often embedded within planning and impact assessment (Taylor, Hobson Bryan, & Goodrich, 1990).

Consequently, in this paper, we explore whether ecological and indeed sociological conceptualizations of resilience can genuinely inform SA and SIA, and hence, social adaptation to climate change. We attempt this by analyzing the ecological, social and psychological literature on resilience. We then explore how some of these concepts might become more useful in the context of climate-related decision making via improved SA/SIA.

2. The origin of social resilience concepts

In the ecological literature, resilience and related concepts are conceptualized in a number of ways according to the different disciplines, contexts and scales. Resilience is variously defined as resisting change (Holling, 1973; Timmerman, 1981), bouncing back (Walker et al., 2004), or transforming (Paton & Johnston, 2006) in response to environmental or social perturbations, or even a combination of these (United Nations International Strategy for Disaster Reduction, 2002). Consistent with the view that it is transformative and/or adaptive, resilience is also viewed as a process (Norris, Stevens, Pfefferbaum, Wyche, & Pfefferbaum, 2008).

These original conceptualizations of ecological resilience logically influenced adaptive management thinking for ecological systems. Such approaches, best known through the work of Holling (1973) were related to theories of resilience which appeared to explore the concept in terms of stability within ecosystems. In line with Holling's work, adaptive management emerged as a 'method to probe the dynamics and resilience of systems while continuing with "management" via management experiments developed to enhance learning and reduce uncertainty' (Holling, 1973 reviewed in Allen, Fontaine, Pope, & Garmestani, 2011, p. 1340). Walters (1986) later promoted processes of continual learning via designed experiments to reduce uncertainty.

Resilience concepts that emerged in the ecological literature hence provided a foundation for more adaptive approaches to decision-making for systems under stress (e.g., those subject to climate change). With this also emerged a growing interest in understanding what community vulnerability and resilience means for environmental management. However, while environmental policy makers have now embraced these concepts, there is still limited uptake of adaptive management practice, largely for sociological reasons (Allen et al., 2011).

The problem here is that adaptive approaches require information about ecological and social, economic and governance dimensions. To date most approaches for assessing progress towards environmental sustainability have focused on understanding biophysical dimensions, often assuming simple cause/effect relationships among variables. An equal focus on strengthening knowledge about social, economic and institutional dimensions of environmental dilemmas is necessary. In practice, this is hindered by poor integration of sociological concepts and measures for social resilience, the rapid timeframes required for making policy decisions and a need to convert theoretical concepts of social resilience into usable knowledge (Béné et al., 2014; Kulig et al., 2013; Magis, 2010; Ross et al., 2010). In this environment, many ecological researchers/practitioners have adopted the terminology concerning social agenda (e.g., referring to socio-ecological systems), but have not integrated core social science concepts concerning social resilience, particularly the building of human/community agency and the management of power-relations (e.g., Adger, 2000; Davidson, 2010). Hence while ecologically-derived thinking on social resilience and adaptive management has much to offer improved decision-making, it is not conceptually powerful in sociological terms, resulting in limited adoption in climate adaptation planning and impact assessment.

2.1 The social science origins of resilience concepts

In parallel to ecological resilience concepts of socio-ecological systems, there have been several co-evolved disciplinary resilience constructs in the social and psychological sciences. These range from the individual psychological scales to concepts of institutional/community resilience. These concepts have evolved separately from the ecological literature and tend to be less focused on informing linear or rational decision-making on climate adaptation.

In the literature, the scales at which social adaptation is considered include the individual/psychological (Barton, 2005; Rutter, 1987), organizations/institutions (Dalziell & Mcmanus, 2004; Gibson & Tarrant, 2010) and community (Gow & Paton, 2008; Handmer & Dovers, 2007).

In considering social resilience, it is important to remember that individual and household resilience in some cases can be linked to community-scale resilience (Boon, Millar, Lake, Cottrell, & King, 2012; Buikstra et al., 2010; Gow & Paton, 2008). An individual's resilience, which has been shown to be a process arising from contextual social, environmental and economic factors (Tusaie & Dyer, 2004), and can contribute to community resilience at an aggregate scale. Social resilience at both scales has also repeatedly been found to rest on relationships between the various levels of social scale; individual, household, organization, community and society (Aldrich, 2012; Luthar, 2006).

In this context, the concept of disaster-based recovery is important: how well do people and social institutions and structures bounce back from challenge (Masten, 2001; Rutter, 1987)? There is some consensus in the social science literature that people who are resilient display a greater capacity to quickly regain equilibrium physiologically, psychologically and socially following stressful events. Within this, the concept of human adaptability is important: the capacity to continue forward in the face of adversity (Bonanno, 2004; Magis, 2010). This is a particularly important aspect of social resilience especially in the face of climate change and the expected attendant natural disasters. Healthy, adaptive communities confer a capacity for resilience to their constituents and vice-versa.

In contrast to individual resilience, community-scale social resilience is described differently in various studies and defined more loosely (Kulig, 2000). Moreover, there is limited empirical data to inform our knowledge of community-scale social resilience. In general, descriptions take three different forms: (1) resistance, which refers to the ability of a community to absorb perturbation (Geis, 2000); (2) recovery, which focuses on the speed and ability to recover from the stressors (Adger, 2000); and (3) creativity, which addresses the ability of a social system to maintain a constant process of creating and recreating, so that the community not only responds to adversity, but in doing so, reaches a higher level of functioning (Kulig & Hanson, 1996).

Adger (2000) defines community-scale social resilience as the ability of communities to withstand external shocks to their social infrastructure. Like 'individual resilience', it must account for the economic, institutional, social and ecological dimensions of a community. Community-scale resilience is hence related to the overall population and its stability and it is integrally linked to individual resilience, with the temporal scale playing a prominent role.

The literature centered on social resilience to disasters enhances our understanding of resilience to climate change since weather-induced disasters are likely to be exacerbated through climate change. In this context, Norris et al. (2008) assert that community resilience is a process and they argue that the concepts apply equally well to most types of collective stressors. They also cite evidence that disaster location (developed country, developing country) is a stronger predictor of sample-level effects than either disaster type (mass violence, natural, technological) or sample type (child, adult, rescue/recovery) (Norris et al., 2008). They describe two approaches evident in the literature: social resilience that prevents disaster-related health problems of community members, and social resilience as it applies to effective organizational behavior and disaster management. Berkes et al. (2003) also argue that social resilience involves a set of adaptive capacities and that it is a strategy for promoting effective disaster readiness and response, maintaining community sustainability.

Sociological concepts of resilience are also related to vulnerability, but rather than being seen as opposite ends of a spectrum, they can be envisaged as parallel sets of indicators. Whereas vulnerability measures susceptibility, resilience draws on the strengths and capacity of people and communities. People's resilience is juxtaposed against their potential vulnerability (Buckle, 2006; Gow & Paton, 2008; Paton, Millar, & Johnston, 2001). Community sustainability also relates to resilience because its purpose is to maintain a working ecosystem that will sustain communities and their resource use into future generations. Many of the things human beings do, however, are not sustainable when confronted by the impacts of climate change (Intergovernmental Panel on Climate Change, 2007). Mitigating climate disasters thus demands change in our economy, resource use patterns, governance and social priorities and relationships. Consequently, the need for adaptation appears inevitable, but understanding capacity for adaptation requires recognition that many factors operating at multiple scales influence vulnerability, resilience and adaptation (Gow & Paton, 2008).

While the above suggests there is considerable sociological literature of relevance to the climate adaptation debate, this literature has been focused on building an understanding of responses to disasters, and not strongly focused on guiding sociologically informed decision-making for community and regional adaptation. Doing so would mean these concepts need to influence and inform the common practice of SA/SIA; the core social methods informing decision-making on adaptation (Becker, 2003). This suggests that to assess whether social resilience definitions are accurate, ways of measuring such resilience must be available. In this context, and at any scale, social resilience needs to be able to be assessed via direct or proxy indicators, such as institutional change, economic structure and demographic change.

3. Can social resilience concepts inform social assessment/social impact assessment for climate change adaptation?

While the sociological literature provides a deeper understanding of social and community resilience, vulnerability and adaptation concepts, it is the ecological literature that more boldly suggests that understanding social resilience might assist with informing decision-making and adaptive management context (Allen et al., 2011; Plummer & Armitage, 2007). In the sociological literature, however, it is to the SA/SIA schools of thought that most concern themselves with arming decision-makers with the evidence required. SA/SIA has had as its primary concern, the pre-empting of social impacts in planning and major project approval processes to determine positive, neutral and negative outcomes of a given project or proposal (Bowles, 1981; Vanclay & Esteves, 2011). Surprisingly, however, the SA/SIA literature does not have a strong tradition of encouraging or underpinning adaptive management approaches. Nor, to date, has it been well informed by social resilience concepts. While Powell and Jiggins (2003) advocate the integration of resilience as a conceptual advance in SIA practice, practical approaches are only just emerging (e.g., Maguire & Cartwright, 2008; World Bank, 2011).

Despite Barrow (2000, p. 2) viewing SIA as 'a systematic, iterative, ideally ex-ante, assessment' of 'change in people's lives brought about by a given action or actions', the SA/SIA literature has tended to evolve largely within technocratic and expert decision-making frameworks. As such, it has a tendency to be linear in its approaches (Becker, 2003; Burdge, 2004) and these are typically applied in practical climate adaptation planning and decision-making. Hence most SA/SIA frameworks tend to be about ensuring the full range of both technical and values-driven data sets are fed to the critical decision-makers seeking to manage the potential impacts of change. There has, however, been an active debate in the literature concerning technical versus political approaches to SA/SIA (Lane, Ross, & Dale, 1997). While more technical approaches are designed to support centralized or rational forms of decision-making, more political and community-based approaches to SA/SIA aim to explicitly inform more equitable socio-political processes within society by empowering the agency of groups more likely to be impacted by change. Such approaches could be very well serviced by greater interaction with the sociological and psychological literature concerning resilience.

While more political forms of SA/SIA are best suited to more integrated, collaborative and adaptive forms of planning, by and large, the SA/SIA literature has tended to align itself more to linear or positivistic forms of decision-making. For this reason, researchers such as Ross and McGee (2006) have been calling for more effort to reconceptualize SA/SIA concepts to make them more relevant to modern thinking about societal decision-making.

Within both the technical and political applications of SA/SIA, however, there has been a consistent recognition of the need to cluster certain categories of social and economic information to improve both impact prediction and decision-making. This approach was popularized by Blishen, Lockhart, Craib, and Lockhart (1979) and Bowles (1981) and can be found in several different conceptualizations of the SA/SIA method (Ross & Mcgee, 2006). Some of these broad information clusters include concepts of social vitality, economic viability and political efficacy (Dale et al., 2011; Maclean et al., 2013). Information clusters of this kind have subsequently informed the development of indicators of relevance to the measurement of social resilience at different scales. Hence the SA/SIA literature suggests that key indicators of resilience can be actively used to help decision-makers conceptualize potential impacts, define adaptation strategies and monitor changes. Thus, while the more political approaches are still not mainstream SA/SIA practice, evidence based approaches to understanding resilience, combined with more coordinated and well facilitated political approaches, offer opportunities to better use social resilience concepts to effectively respond to climate change. This complements calls from the ecological resilience literature for a shift to more collaborative and adaptive decision-making (Bardsley & Rogers, 2010; Loring, Gerlach, Atkinson, & Murray, 2011).

Consequently, if communities/societies at any scale deserve evidence-based support to help make decisions about climate adaptation, then we suggest that it is possible to use the strengths and avoid the weaknesses of all three intellectual traditions (ecological concepts of adaptive management, sociological and psychological concepts of social resilience and the decision-informing power of SA/SIA). To do this, we are suggesting:

(1) That the disciplinary approaches of the social science literature in defining and articulating what resilience means in an individual and community context be better accepted;

(2) That the SA/SIA intellectual traditions tell us that sociological evidence can and should better inform (both technical and political forms of) decision-making; and

(3) That the premise from the ecological resilience literature that decision-making should consider social evidence in more adaptive/collaborative decision-making be accepted.

Individually, all three intellectual traditions have their weaknesses. Combined, they deliver some confidence that SA, SIA and resilience concepts can genuinely inform community adaptation to climate change at any scale; but particularly at regional scale. Hence, in the following section, we explore some practical considerations of how these ideas might inform a more effective approach to applying social resilience concepts to climate adaptation.

4. Translating social resilience concepts into SA/SIA for adaptation

Global climate change scenarios denote a long-term, slow-onset change (Hewitt, 1997). This will include regionalized and local responses to a series of episodic disasters. They also have implications for understanding the development and application of resilience concepts to adaptation and suggest that regions could be an important focal scale for adaptation activity. In particular, this means that more adaptive styles of regional decision-making are possible over longer time frames. Because the impacts of climate change are intergenerational, intensely social approaches are required if regional and local communities are to support the development and implementation of adaptation strategies. At the same time, there are intense and urgent demands to proactively deal with the potential social and community impacts of extreme episodic events and ecological thresholds surpassed as a result of climate change.

Hence, the above challenges us to think about how to best operationalize social resilience concepts for enhanced SA within adaptive planning processes while at the same time considering more immediate SIA concepts in communities and regions vulnerable to climate change. Consequently, the following explores some of the challenges likely to face the application of social resilience concepts within SA/SIA concerning adaptation planning.

First, it seems that understanding resilience within regional, sub-regional, and local communities in the context of climate change and associated disasters can inform conversations about adaptation. Indeed, knowledge of the dynamic relationships that exist between vulnerability, resilience, hazard impact, hazard change, adaptive capacity and social change in the context of climate change and disasters is a pre-requisite for community-based adaptation. We need to be encouraging such socially informed decision-making at several social scales (from national policy responses to family and enterprise levels).

As mentioned previously though, the problem has been that resilience and related concepts are defined and conceptualized in many different ways according to the different disciplines, problem contexts, scales and objectives (e.g., resisting change, bouncing back, or transforming in response to environmental or social perturbations). This has hindered the effective integration of social resilience concepts into policy and planning interventions. Datasets available to decision-managers to define and measure social resilience, the rapid timeframes required for reviewing and making policy decisions and a need to convert theoretical concepts of social resilience into useful knowledge have all been hindrances.

Hence there are several problems that any approach seeking to operationalize concepts of social resilience at regional levels need to overcome. Firstly resources for stakeholders and agencies for monitoring and evaluation are often limited. Ad hoc funding for social research generally means the consideration of social resilience is not on parity with ecological research. Decision-makers rarely can collect information against lengthy lists of indicators or usefully interpret them. Simpler frameworks are needed that can assist with the development and use indicators for assessment and benchmarking (e.g., see Maclean et al., 2013). This means that the use data and indicators need to be relevant to the context and readily understood. Data should not simply be used or applied simply because it is readily available.

Secondly, employing indicators as part of an overall assessment of social resilience raises methodological questions about how to assess thresholds of resilience (Christensen & Krogman, 2012; Davidson, 2010). At what point can communities and regions be considered socially resilient? The relative bearing of different indicators on actual social resilience and the interplay between different indicators and thresholds remains poorly defined. The interplay of resilience factors across spatial scales (e.g., individual, household and community/region) is also not well understood.

Consequently, research has struggled to find suitable ways to assess social resilience. The two dominant approaches are: (1) generalized measures that integrate data into composite indices; and (2) approaches that pursue multiple lines of evidence. Generalized measures use composite indices to reduce all variables to one number in order to provide data that is temporally and spatially comparable (Adger, Brooks, Bentham, Agnew, & Eriksen, 2004; Cutter, Burton, & Emrich, 2010; Rygel, O'sullivan, & Yarnal, 2006). Advantages of composite indices include their standardized approach to assessment within and across regions and over time. Disadvantages lie in the dynamic nature of relationships between different aspects of resilience which can affect the overall status of a system. A composite value, for example, could indicate that a region is not vulnerable when it may in fact be extremely vulnerable because of a single critical factor (Rygel et al., 2006). Such approaches also require significant resources to identify relevant metrics and data.

Thirdly, information derived from such assessments also needs to be effectively integrated into decision-making. Research often generates information that stakeholders cannot interpret within the context of existing governance arrangements. Hezri and Dovers (2009, p. 312) describe how the interest in indicator based systems 'draws from the belief that research, statistics and indicators can lead to policies that will work better, on the assumption that "scientific" information could guide social affairs'. In real terms, however, lack of attention to consolidating multiple indicator systems into useful information restricts their use in policy and planning. Stakeholders can have trouble translating copious amounts of information into something meaningful for decision-making (Hezri & Dovers, 2009).

Finally, the implications for SA/SIA are that there is a need to view the assessment process as broader than a technical, linear process primarily devoted to assessing project or program activities (Vanclay & Esteves, 2011). Issues of climate change and social uncertainty due to uncertain climatic conditions require assessment processes that envision a longer time frame and that involve community participation processes. In particular, more attention to geography/location and political processes is required (Béné et al., 2014).

5. Conclusions

This paper has explored the potential application of social resilience concepts within decision-making for climate change adaptation at region scale. Our main conclusion is that a stronger framework for the application of social resilience informed by social science concepts is required within the improved application of SA/SIA within adaptive planning approaches to climate change adaptation. Doing so could deliver powerful information into decision-making processes that allow stakeholders to judge whether policy arrangements governing adaptation to climate change are effectively meeting the needs of the community and the environment over time. If included in long-term social and ecological monitoring programs within climate-vulnerable regions, regions could better qualify, and perhaps quantify, the impact of changing climate and extreme climatic events while also maintaining or improving economic and social wellbeing and the health of the natural resource base.

We find that while the ecological resilience literature champions the idea of integrating social resilience concepts within adaptive management regimes, we concur with others that there has been an intellectual disconnect between the sociologically- and psychologically-based social resilience literature and the biophysically-based concepts concerning the function of socio-ecological systems. There has also been a disconnect between the more positivist SA and SIA literature, the social resilience literature and ecological concepts of adaptive management.

Viewed collectively, however, all three intellectual traditions add value to the business of regional-scale adaptation to climate change. The call from the ecological literature for consideration of social resilience concepts is legitimate, but needs to be serviced more by the socio-psychological discourse on resilience. Social resilience concepts must also better inform the SA/SIA discourse that underpins planning and decision-making for adaptation. Finally, through referring more to the adaptive management literature, SA/SIA methods can be modified to better support adaptive versus linear forms of decision-making.

Acknowledgements

This work was funded by the Queensland Government through the Queensland Centre for Social Science Innovation (QCSSI) and the Northern Futures Collaborative Research Network (CRN). The authors would also specifically like to acknowledge the significant contributions to this work of Ruth Potts (Griffith University), Helen Boon (James Cook University), Bob Stevenson (James Cook University), David King (James Cook University), Margaret Gooch (Great Barrier Reef Marine Park Authority), Hurriyet Babacan (James Cook University) and Bronwyn Voyce (Griffith University).

References

Adger, W. N. (2000). Social and ecological resilience: Are they related? *Progress in Human Geography, 24*(3), 347–364. doi:10.1191/030913200701540465

Adger, W. N., Brooks, N., Bentham, G., Agnew, M., & Eriksen, S. (2004). *New indicators of vulnerability and adaptive capacity*. Norwich, UK: Tyndall Centre for Climate Change Research.

Aldrich, D. P. (2012). *Building resilience: Social capital in post-disaster recovery*. Chicago, IL: The University of Chicago Press.

Allen, C. R., Fontaine, J. J., Pope, K. L., & Garmestani, A. S. (2011). Adaptive management for a turbulent future. *Journal of Environmental Management, 92*(5), 1339–1345. doi:10.1016/j.jenvman.2010.11.019

Bardsley, D. K., & Rogers, G. P. (2010). Prioritizing engagement for sustainable adaptation to climate change: An example from natural resource management in south australia. *Society and Natural Resources, 24*(1), 1–17.

Barrow, C. J. (2000). *Social impact assessment: An introduction*. London: Arnold.

Barton, W. H. (2005). Methodological challenges in the study of resilience. In M. Ungar (Ed.), *Handbook for working with children and youth* (pp. 135–148). London: Sage.

Becker, H. (2003). Theory formation and application in social impact assessment. In H. Becker & F. Vanclay (Eds.), *The international handbook of social impact assessment: Conceptual and methodological advances* (pp. 129–142). Cheltenham, UK: Edward Elgar.

Béné, C., Newsham, A., Davies, M., Ulrichs, M., & Godfrey-Wood, R. (2014). Review article: Resilience, poverty and development. *Journal of International Development, 26*(5): 598–623.

Berkes, F., Colding, J., & Folke, C. (2003). *Navigating social-ecological systems: Building resilience for complexity and change*. New York, NY: Cambridge University Press.

Berkes, F., & Ross, H. (2013). Community resilience: Toward an integrated approach. *Society & Natural Resources, 26*(1), 5–20. doi:10.1080/08941920.2012.736605

Blishen, B., Lockhart, A., Craib, P., & Lockhart, E. (1979). *Socio-economic impact model for northern development*. Hull, UK: Department of Indian and Northern Affairs.

Bonanno, G. A. (2004). Loss, trauma, and human resilience: Have we underestimated the human capacity to thrive after extremely aversive events? *The American Psychologist, 59*(1), 20–28. doi:10.1037/0003-066X.59.1.20

Boon, H. J., Millar, J., Lake, D., Cottrell, A., & King, D. (2012) Recovery From Disaster: Resilience, Adaptability and Perceptions of Climate Change. National Climate change Adaptation Facility Publication Number 26/12. ISBN: 978-1-921609-63-3.

Bowles, R. (1981). *Social impact assessment in small communities: An integrated review of selected literature*. Toronto: Buttersworth.

Brown, K., & Westaway, E. (2011). Agency, capacity, and resilience to environmental change: Lessons from human development, well-being, and disasters. *Annual Review of Environment and Resources, 36*, 321–342.

Buckle, P. (2006). Assessing social resilience. In D. Paton & D. M. Johnston (Eds.), *Disaster resilience: An integrated approach* (pp. 88–103). Springfield, IL: Charles C Thomas.

Buikstra, E., Ross, H., King, C. A., Baker, P. G., Hegney, D., McLachlan, K., & Rogers-Clark, C. (2010). The components of resilience – perceptions of an Australian rural community. *Journal of Community Psychology, 38*(8), 975–991. doi:10.1002/jcop.20409

Burdge, R. (2004). *The concepts, process and methods of social impact assessment*. Middleton WI: Social Ecology Press.

Christensen, L., & Krogman, N. (2012). Social thresholds and their translation into social-ecological management practices. *Ecology and Society, 17*(1), 5. Retrieved from http://www.ecologyand-society.org/vol17/iss1/art5/ 10.5751/ES-04499-170105

Cutter, S. L., Burton, C. G., & Emrich, C. T. (2010). Disaster resilience indicators for benchmarking baseline conditions. *Journal of Homeland Security and Emergency Management, 7*(1), 1–22. doi:10.2202/1547-7355.1732

Dale, A., Taylor, N., & Lane, M. (2001). *Social assessment in natural resource management institutions*. Collingwood, VIC: CSIRO Publishing.

Dale, A., Vella, K., Cottrell, A., Pert, P., Stephenson, B., Boon, H., … Gooch, M. (2011). *Conceptualising, evaluating and reporting social resilience in vulnerable regional and remote communities facing climate change in tropical queensland*. Cairns, QLD: RRRC.

Dalziell, E., & Mcmanus, S. (2004). *Resilience, vulnerability, and adaptive capacity: Implications for system performance*. Christchurch, NZ: University of Canterbury.

Davidson, D. J. (2010). The applicability of the concept of resilience to social systems: Some sources of optimism and nagging doubts. *Society and Natural Resources, 23*(12), 1135–1149. doi:10.1080/08941921003652940

Folke, C. (2006). Resilience: The emergence of a perspective for social–ecological systems analyses. *Global Environmental Change, 16*(3), 253–267. doi:10.1016/j.gloenvcha.2006.04.002

Geis, D. E. (2000). By design: The disaster resistant and quality-of-life community. *Natural Hazards Review, 1*(3), 151–160. doi:10.1061/(ASCE)1527-6988(2000)1:3(151)

Gibson, C. A., & Tarrant, M. (2010). A conceptual models approach to organisational resilience. *Australian Journal of Emergency Management, 25*(2), 6–12.

Gooch, M., & Rigano, D. (2010). Enhancing community-scale social resilience: What is the connection between healthy communities and healthy waterways? *Australian Geographer, 41*(4), 507–520. doi:10.1080/00049182.2010.519698

Gow, K., & Paton, D. (2008). Rising from the ashes: Empowering the phoenix. In K. Gow & D. Paton (Eds.), *The phoenix of natural disasters: Community resilience* (pp. 1–9). New York, NY: Nova Science Publishers.

Handmer, J. W., & Dovers, S. (2007). *The handbook of disaster and emergency policies and institutions*. London: Earthscan.

Hare, W. L., Cramer, W., Schaeffer, M., Battaglini, A., & Jaeger, C. C. (2011). Climate hotspots: Key vulnerable regions, climate change and limits to warming. *Regional Environmental Change, 11*(1), 1–13. doi:10.1007/s10113-010-0195-4

Hewitt, K. (1997). *Regions of risk: A geographical introduction to disasters*. Harlow: Longman.

Hezri, A. A., & Dovers, S. R. (2009). Australia's indicator-based sustainability assessments and public policy. *Australian Journal of Public Administration, 68*(3), 303–318.

Holling, C. S. (1973). Resilience and stability of ecological systems. *Annual Review of Ecology and Systematics, 4*(1), 1–23. doi:10.1146/annurev.es.04.110173.000245

Intergovernmental Panel on Climate Change. (2007). *Climate change 2007: Synthesis report.* Geneva: IPCC.

Kulig, J., & Hanson, L. (1996). *Discussion and expansion of the concept of resiliency: Summary of a think tank.* Lethbridge, Alberta: Regional centre for health promotion and community studies, University of Lethbridge.

Kulig, J. C. (2000). Community resiliency: The potential for community health nursing theory development. *Public Health Nursing, 17*(5), 374–385. doi:10.1046/j.1525-1446.2000.00374.x

Kulig, J. C., Edge, D. ,S., Townshend, I., Lightfoot, N., & Reimer, W. (2013). Community resiliency: Emerging theoretical insights. *Journal of Community Psychology, 41*(6), 758–775. doi:10.1002/jcop.21569

Lane, M. B., Ross, H., & Dale, A. P. (1997). Social impact research: Integrating the technical, political, and planning paradigms. *Human Organization, 56*(3), 302.

Loring, P. A., Gerlach, C., Atkinson, D. E., & Murray, M. S. (2011). Ways to help and ways to hinder: Governance for effective adaptation to an uncertain climate. *Arctic, 64*(1), 73–88. doi:10.14430/arctic4081

Luthar, S. S. (2006). Resilience in development: A synthesis of research across five decades. In D. Cicchetti & D. J. Cohen (Eds.), *Developmental psychopathology, volume 3, risk, disorder, and adaptation* (2nd ed., pp. 739–795). Hoboken NJ: John Wiley & Sons.

Maclean, K., Cuthill, M., & Ross, H. (2013). Six attributes of social resilience. *Journal of Environmental Planning and Management, 57*(1), 1–13.

Magis, K. (2010). Community resilience: An indicator of social sustainability. *Society & Natural Resources: An International Journal, 23*(5), 401–416.

Maguire, B., & Cartwright, S. (2008). *Assessing a community's capacity to manage change: A resilience approach to social assessment.* Canberra: Bureau of Rural Sciences.

Masten, A. S. (2001). Ordinary magic: Resilience processes in development. *American Psychologist, 56*(3), 227–238. doi:10.1037/0003-066X.56.3.227

Norris, F. H., Stevens, S. P., Pfefferbaum, B., Wyche, K. F., & Pfefferbaum, R. L. (2008). Community resilience as a metaphor, theory, set of capacities, and strategy for disaster readiness. *American Journal of Community Psychology, 41*(1–2), 127–150. doi:10.1007/s10464-007-9156-6

Paton, D., & Johnston, D. M. (2006). *Disaster resilience: An integrated approach.* Springfield, IL: Charles C Thomas.

Paton, D., Millar, M., & Johnston, D. (2001). Community resilience to volcanic hazard consequences. *Natural Hazards, 24*(2), 157–169. doi:10.1023/A:1011882106373

Plummer, R., & Armitage, D. (2007). A resilience-based framework for evaluating adaptive co-management: Linking ecology, economics and society in a complex world. *Ecological Economics, 61*(1), 62–74. doi:10.1016/j.ecolecon.2006.09.025

Powell, N., & Jiggins, J. (2003). Learning from participatory land management. In H. A. Becker & F. Vanclay (Eds.), *The international handbook of social impact assessment* (pp. 42–55). Cheltenham, UK: Edward Elgar.

Ross, H., & Mcgee, T. (2006). Conceptual frameworks for SIA revisited: A cumulative effects study on lead contamination and economic change. *Impact Assessment and Project Appraisal, 24*(2), 139–149. doi:10.3152/147154606781765273

Ross, H., Cuthill, M., Maclean, K., Jansen, D., & Witt, B. (2010). *Understanding, enhancing and managing for social resilience at the regional scale: Opportunities in north queensland. Report to the marine and tropical sciences research facility* (186 pp.). Cairns: Reef and Rainforest Research Centre Limited.

Rutter, M. (1987). Psychosocial resilience and protective mechanisms. *American Journal of Orthopsychiatry, 57*(3), 316–331. doi:10.1111/j.1939-0025.1987.tb03541.x

Rygel, L., O'sullivan, D., & Yarnal, B. (2006). A method for constructing a social vulnerability index: An application to hurricane storm surges in a developed country. *Mitigation and Adaptation Strategies for Global Change, 11*(3), 741–764. doi:10.1007/s11027-006-0265-6

Stanley, J. (2010). *Promoting social inclusion in adaptation to climate change: Discussion paper.* Melbourne, Victoria: Department of Sustainability and Environment.

Taylor, N. C., Hobson Bryan, C., & Goodrich, C. G. (1990). *Social assessment: Theory, process and techniques.* Canterbury: Centre of Resource Management.

Timmerman, P. (1981). *Vulnerability, resilience and the collapse of society: A review of models and possible climatic applications.* Toronto: Institute for Environmental Studies, University of Toronto.

Tusaie, K., & Dyer, J. (2004). Resilience: A historical review of the construct. *Holistic Nursing Practice, 18*(1), 3–10. doi:10.1097/00004650-200401000-00002

United Nations International Strategy for Disaster Reduction. (2002). *Living with risk: A global review of disaster risk reduction initiatives*. Geneva, Switzerland: ISDR Secretariat.

Vanclay, F. & Esteves, M. A. (Eds.). (2011). *New directions in social impact assessment: Conceptual and methodological advances*. Elwood, IN: Edgar Elwood Publishing.

Walker, B., Hollin, C. S., Carpenter, S. R., & Kinzig, A. (2004). Resilience, adaptability and transformability in social-ecological systems. *Ecology and Society, 9*(2), 5–5.

Walters, C. J. (1986). *Adaptive management of renewable resources*. New York, NY: Macmillan.

World Bank. (2011). *Social resilience and climate change: Operational toolkit*. Washington: World Bank.

Index

accountability 47
adaptability 95, 96
agricultural inter-generational decision making
model 71–92; household consumption
outcomes 86–7, 88; household earnings 78;
human capital accumulation 72–3, 74, 77,
82–3, 86, 87; networking 78, 85–6; social
capital 78–9, 85, 89
Australia, droughts 71–2

capacity building 1, 2, 6, 10; *see also* resilience
concepts
Census place 11
Charles River basin 23–4, 27–8, 33, 37, 38
climate change 2, 4, 47, 53, 71–3, 88, 90, 94,
97; adaptation to 97–9; Intergovernmental
Panel on Climate Change 2
collaboration: benefits 54–5, 58–63; flood
forecasting 46; Provider-User Matrix 55–67
collaborative planning 54
communicative rationality 54
community adaptation 93, 94, 96, 97–100;
see also resilience concepts
Community Ratings System 3, 5–22
Connecticut River basin 28, 33–4
Corps of Engineers 23–40; cost-benefit
analyses 25–6, 30–5; as land protection
agency 35–7
Cragg model 16, 17

decision making model, inter-generational
71–92
decision support technologies 45
deterministic forecasting 43, 47
droughts 2, 4; government response 71–2;
groundwater loss 80–1; groundwater
outcomes 84; inter-generational decision
making model 71–92

ecological resilience 94, 95, 98, 101; *see also*
resilience concepts
educational attainment 10, 11, 16, 18, 19, 72,
74, 76–7; *see also* human capital
accumulation

ensemble forecast systems 3, 42, 43, 46;
see also probabilistic forecasting
European Flood Alert System (EFAS) 47

flood disaster management 2, 3; data
analysis 12; data gathering 11–12; literature
review 8–10; political-economy factors 11;
results 12–16; risk factors 10, 18; socio-
demographic factors 11; Special Flood
Hazard Areas 7, 8; US Community Ratings
System 3, 5–22; variables 12, 13
flood risk management *see* risk management
floodplains 5, 7, 14, 24; building in 20;
conservation 23–40; mapping 9, 46
forecasts *see* probabilistic forecasting

'green' flood control 23–40
green infrastructure 38

Habermas, Jürgen 54
hazard mitigation 9, 18, 41, 46
human capital accumulation 72–3, 74, 77, 82–3,
86, 87; innate learning capability 77
hydrometeorological forecasting *see*
probabilistic forecasting
Hyogo Framework 2

India, droughts 72
institutional design 1, 3
inter-generational decision making model
71–92
Intergovernmental Panel on Climate Change
(IPCC) 2

Koontz, Thomas M 55

land acquisition 23, 24, 28, 29, 31–3, 35–7
land protection 35–7
Ljusnan River Group, Sweden 57–65;
provider-assessed benefits 60–3; Provider-
User Matrix 63–5; user-assessed benefits
62–3

Millennium Development Plan 2

For Product Safety Concerns and Information please contact our EU
representative GPSR@taylorandfrancis.com Taylor & Francis Verlag GmbH,
Kaufingerstraße 24, 80331 München, Germany

Batch number: 08153807

Printed by Printforce, the Netherlands